WALK IN BALANCE

Also by Lynn Andrews

Crystal Woman
Flight of the Seventh Moon
Jaguar Woman
The Mask of Power
Medicine Woman
The Power Deck
Shakkai, Woman of the Sacred Garden
Star Woman
Teachings Around the Sacred Wheel
Windhorse Woman
Woman at the Edge of Two Worlds
The Woman of Wyrrd

WALK IN BALANCE

MEDITATIONS WITH LYNN ANDREWS

Lynn V. Andrews

HarperSanFrancisco
A Division of HarperCollins*Publishers*

Grateful acknowledgment is made to the following for permission to quote from previously published material:

To HarperCollins Publishers for excerpts from *Medicine Woman* copyright © 1981 by Lynn Andrews Productions, Inc., *Flight of the Seventh Moon* copyright © 1984 by Lynn Andrews Productions, Inc., *Jaguar Woman* copyright © 1985 by Lynn Andrews Productions, Inc., *Teachings Around the Sacred Wheel* copyright © 1989 by Lynn Andrews Productions, Inc., *The Woman of Wyrrd* copyright © 1990 by Lynn Andrews Productions, Inc., *The Power Deck* copyright © 1991 by Lynn Andrews Productions, Inc., *The Mask of Power* copyright © 1992 by Lynn Andrews Productions, Inc., *Shakkai* copyright © 1993 by Lynn Andrews Productions, Inc., and *Woman at the Edge of Two Worlds* copyright © 1993 by Lynn Andrews Productions, Inc. Reprinted by permission.

To Warner Books for excerpts from *Crystal Woman* copyright © 1987 by Lynn Andrews, *Star Woman* copyright © 1987 by Lynn Andrews, and *Windhorse Woman* copyright © 1989 by Lynn Andrews. Reprinted by permission of Warner Books/New York.

This book is dedicated

to the memory of

Nellie Duckworth

And special appreciation for

their energy and insight to

Tom Grady and Caroline Pincus

of Harper San Francisco

If you want power, you have to make a place inside you for power to live.

Grandmother
Woman at the Edge of Two Worlds

Introduction

This book of meditations will give you something new to think about, something new to focus on, every day. After you read your daily affirmation, walk into your day imbued with a sense of power. The thoughts that mark each day will lead you to a centering place within yourself, so that when you go out into the world, you will go from a stance of power, with a sense of your own personal truth. If you read these affirmations at night before you sleep, they will help you to move into your dreams with thoughts of something other than the troubles of your day. They will allow you to explore new realities and dimensions of thought that perhaps would not come to you on your own.

I wanted to compile this book of meditations because so often we look at a calendar of days as merely a symbol of the passage of time. We forget why we are on this earth. We forget that there is a reason for all of the pain and all of the struggle. We forget that we were put on this earth to learn something. If everything were perfect in this life, we would never learn anything new. We would not be able to elevate our spirits through the events that happen to us.

These teachings are dialogues from many, many years of my work with Agnes Whistling Elk, Ruby Plenty Chiefs, and the extraordinary women of the Sisterhood of the Shields. Just as these teachings come down to us through many years and through the seasons of our lives, so the book is organized according to the seasons of the year.

The spring teachings are about planting the seeds of new ideas and new endeavors and discovering new clarity in your life. They involve healing the child within.

The summer is about the seed coming into full growth, the flowering of your thoughts—in essence, the adolescence and young adulthood of your spirit and your life process.

Fall is a time of gathering. You have flowered, you have grown, and now you begin to gather food for the long winter, food for thought. You take stock of what you have, of what you have encountered. You bring even more clarity and focus into your acts of power. Autumn is the season of your adult within. It is a time for celebrating what you have become.

The winter teachings are about taking what you have gathered into your mental and spiritual cave of hibernation and circling around the teachings that you have received. You carefully turn over each word and idea, perhaps digesting them for the first time, truly metabolizing them into your life, to be expressed anew in the spring. Winter is a time of regeneration, a time where the seeds are harvested and put into the seed banks of your subconscious mind to be given to future generations, to be given back to yourself when they are needed. It is the season of the grandparents, the old wise ones within.

Walk in balance with one foot in your spiritual understanding and one foot in your physical world of accomplishment. I present these daily empowerments to you as a gift from my heart, just as they were a profound gift of experience from my teachers. The process of going back through my books, which represent my life journey toward enlightenment, was very exciting to me; I had never looked at the teachings as separate from my experience.

I offer you this book of meditations with great respect for your commitment to your own acts of power. I offer it with my prayers that your year will be filled with light and with powerful mirrors to reflect your personal journey.

Walk in balance all the days of your life.

In Spirit,

Lynn Andrews

Remember that the flight is forever. Enjoy it.

Agnes Whistling Elk
Jaguar Woman

January 1

The Universe Within

Everything comes from nothing. Our universe is magnificent in its manifestations of power, but when you go to the center, when you go to the beginning of things, you move, not out into the world for your instruction, but to the interior world, the universe that lives within. It is from the essence of that universe that all life is born.

Agnes Whistling Elk
Shakkai, Woman of the Sacred Garden

January 2

Stand in the Center of Your Knowing

You don't know what you are. There is no explaining why you are born, or why you are the animated part of the earth that you are. You think that I don't know you or anything about you. But I can tell you an experience that you had. I've never seen the great lakes of this world, the ocean. But I can tell you that one day the water washed over you. So the womb of this world has chosen you and given you protection. That was a power sign to you, a gift from the womb of your mother, the earth, and that is why the dreamers have reached you. There is no explaining why you have been chosen. All that is left for you is the knowing.

Agnes Whistling Elk
Medicine Woman

January 3

Melt into Enlightenment

We come into this earthwalk for only one reason. This turtle island is a great schoolhouse. We have chosen to come here only to become one with the Great Spirit. In your words, to become enlightened. Yet it's the one thing we're most afraid of. You come here like everyone else. Like an ice cube trying to melt into the all-surrounding ocean of enlightenment. But how do you do that? You come to a teacher. And that teacher holds up a mirror. And if you're willing to look into it, the mirror becomes like the sun and you begin to heat up. You begin to melt into that ocean.

Agnes Whistling Elk
Star Woman

January 4

Bliss

When we enter the void, it's like no place we have ever been before. Some people see angels; some see warriors. Some call these beings gods and goddesses. Some call them spirits.

Agnes Whistling Elk
Jaguar Woman

January 5

A Place of Witnessing

The sacred Tao is already within you. You do not want to stay in school forever. You need to move on, and the more you try to make this life a fixture, something you can hang on to, the more it will disappoint you. There is no way to make anything in this life substantial enough to depend upon. It simply is not the nature of this life, and you are fooling yourself if you think otherwise. The only permanence in this life is your sacred witness, that place of power and emptiness within you which watches the unfolding of time forever. That place of witnessing, in truth, is all that any of us have. And the wisdom that you bring to that watching, to that place of power, is the imprint that is left on your spirit shield, and it shows that you have lived the goodness of your heart.

Shakkai
Shakkai, Woman of the Sacred Garden

Listen for Guidance

Lynn, you've tripped over an eagle feather as if it were blocking your path. An eagle soars above and sees all the vast complexities and interrelationships. When an eagle feather falls from a medicine eagle to the earth, it is full of that knowledge. If you're smart, you will talk to that eagle feather and ask the spirit of it to guide you. All eagle feathers have that power. You have to pick it up and talk to it. Then you have to know how to listen to the answer.

Agnes Whistling Elk
Medicine Woman

January 7

Confront Your Pain

You learned to study your own suffering so that the suffering of others could be understood. Teach your apprentices not to distract themselves from their pain. Lead them into the center of pain, to confront it.

Ginevee
Crystal Woman

January 8

All There Is

"But what does it really mean to be enlightened?"

"I like to describe it like this," Shakkai said. "Think of the light within you. Think of the radiance that you are, that we all are, and think of death, when your body lies down and goes back into the earth, into the sacred mountain. What is left?"

"The light?" I replied.

"Yes, the light. It is never-ending, and it goes back to its source. That light is purely of the sacredness of life, and it goes back to God, it goes back to the Tao. It is the Tao. It is the Great Spirit. You are the Great Spirit. And that's really all there is."

O Kiku and Shakkai
Shakkai, Woman of the Sacred Garden

January 9

Shaman Will

Your shaman will has brought you to this point of power. It is time now to let your will rest. We are the stars in one another's universe forever.

Agnes Whistling Elk
The Woman of Wyrrd

January 10

Omens Are Promises

I would like to leave you with a present, Lynn, an idea. The omens are promises, but only if you follow them. For instance, let's say that I would like to give you not only a present, but something to think about as well. I see my history and my vision in a horse's eyes. Each shaman has a secret. All of her energy comes from her myth. My myth is the image of the horse, which to me is freedom. There is freedom in the sound of the hooves carrying me through space and time and other dimensions of reality. When I become the horse, I am created from thunder and lightning. I reclaim the horse. I participate in that plane of sympathetic magic. I am the apocalyptic energy of horse, of life and death. As a horse gallops, I, too, approach you as in the ceaseless movement of the ocean's waves.

Twin Dreamers
Star Woman

January 11

Believe in Magic

It is important to understand the value of realizing your dreams in life. Remember that this is done without manipulating or hurting anyone around you. It is a healing path, and it is a path of love. But it is also a magical path, and for magic to happen in your life, you must believe in magic.

Grandmother
The Woman of Wyrrd

January 12
Honor the Dark Side

If you do not honor the dark side, then you will be ruled by the dark side. You must look at it and understand it, and then turn your face away and let the light be your guide. To understand the darkness does not mean you become it. Examine it carefully, knowing what it is made of, understanding its power and its limitations.

Shakkai
Shakkai, Woman of the Sacred Garden

January 13
Kinship

My mind followed a labyrinth of symbols, images, and primeval ideas, each somehow more fascinating than the last, yet behind each a terrible, aching loneliness. How few people ever surrender to a feeling of love, know it, breathe it. And now out of that dark, karmic wheel, a bridge was being formed. I knew from that moment forward I would always know my kinship with these women. They were my sisterhood. I had found my circle.

Lynn
Flight of the Seventh Moon

January 14
Live Your Truth

The truth is within your own heart and your own soul. When you become lonely and afraid, all the answers you will ever need will be found within yourself. Do not look so frantically out into the world for the answers to your questions. Look within, and ask yourself, "Am I being faithful to my own truth?" Losing that faith is the only real sin against the Goddess Mother. We forget who we are in this world of illusion. And it is the one thing that we must forgive and cure. The Old One will survive in all of her women.

Grandmother
The Woman of Wyrrd

January 15

You Are a Keeper of Earth Wisdom

Life is a planting of the spirit so that a body can be formed from the dying seed. The monsters you have seen are the bardos, or stages of life, that you have lived on this earth. Without this earth, the seeds of the spirit would have no place to be born. You are a keeper of this mother garden. The wisdom will remain safe here.

Windhorse
Windhorse Woman

January 16

In Form

Lynn, you often speak of "karma." If a great teacher chooses to stay on this earth to teach, she may take on karma in order to stay in form. Once you release the mind from karma, you have the ability to step out of time into formlessness. That is the law of doubling, the process of remirroring from one round to another. Leaping over karma, you are able to be in more places than one. The world hasn't changed. Your self lodge has. Why do you suppose you see great women or men of knowledge who have addictions to alcohol or food? Because addictions are karma, and they keep you nailed down on this earthly plane. They keep you in form.

Agnes Whistling Elk
Jaguar Woman

January 17

Find Your Essence

Perhaps if you find the core of your existence, the Godness inside you, the Great Mother inside you, perhaps it would be nothing except the spirit, the essence. And when you find that essence, you can move that essence into any shape that you desire.

Grandmother
The Woman of Wyrrd

Merge into One Being

I was possessed by love for the Kokopelli, and we were performing a sacred ceremony that would bring power to the everlasting flow of life. I was the symbol of all women. His face glowed—changing, disappearing, reappearing. I closed my eyes and became aware of what was neither him nor me, but the power of the dream that stood behind us both. It was a union of the higher and lower selves and we were made one with all cosmic life. The flute seemed to play on by itself. As we lay on the stone altar, the hot night breeze blowing over us like an astral blanket, I looked up into the face of the Kokopelli and realized that I lay there alone—that by possessing him whom I had feared and wanted most, we had merged into one being, warrior and warrioress. I had mated with the warrior—the male—in myself.

Lynn
Medicine Woman

January 19

Fear Is a Tracker

Fear is a shape-shifter's biggest enemy. You must never run from fear. You must face it. Fear is a tracker that will hunt you down. He shoots his arrows just as you leap from one dream form into the other.

> Twin Dreamers
> *Star Woman*

January 20

Be Attentive

As above, so below. The important thing is to be serious, to be attentive, to let your knowing be balanced with substance.

> Agnes Whistling Elk
> *Flight of the Seventh Moon*

January 21

You Are a Being of Stealth

A being of stealth is a credible being. A being of stealth can enter a room and do what she wants. She can leave the room when she wants to. Most beings who enter a room are led and confused, but a being of stealth can enter and leave any room that she wants to. A being of stealth is dangerous and not afraid to strike. A stealthy being knows of her own death.

Agnes Whistling Elk
Medicine Woman

January 22

A Teacher Never Shelters You from Experience

You can never tell someone about an experience that she is going to have. You can never tell her how to behave or how not to behave, because then you would be cheating her of that experience.

Grandmother
The Woman of Wyrrd

January 23

Mirrors Don't Lie

Only God is the source, and like a mirror, we are mirror images of God. A mirror enables us to understand the nature of ourselves, of God. That is all. It is a sacred tool, a device for reflection, just as this physical body is a sacred tool or device for the process of evolvement into the higher realms. Our physical existence provides mirrors for learning. A mirror is part of the teaching.

Ani
Windhorse Woman

January 24

Protection from Harm

There is a life force in all of us. The life force comes directly from the Goddess Mother, from God. It is a protection, a shield that protects the body from invasion. When an evil form of a spirit attacks you with arrows of disease and negativity, the life force flames to protect your physical being from onslaught.

Grandmother
The Woman of Wyrrd

January 25

Sacred Clown

They say that a heyoka, a sacred clown, remembers the trail and takes a different one. So? If you meet a heyoka, you want to shut your eyes and quickly walk by, because any confrontation will change your life forever.

Ruby Plenty Chiefs
Flight of the Seventh Moon

January 26

Self-Completion

You find your circle only when you are ready, and no one will ever succeed in this great and worthy struggle without being close to self-completion. Your circle has been calling you since the day of your birth. You have never had the personal power to hear them. You have confronted those in your circle many times in the past, but they were invisible to you. It is your responsibility never to doubt the existence of this sisterhood. Before you can enter and be recognized into your society, you must learn many things. When you join them, they give you gifts and their power becomes your power.

Agnes Whistling Elk
Flight of the Seventh Moon

January 27

The Final Giveaway

When your spirit parts from your body, it is the final giveaway. Your spirit continues to emanate light and strength like the sun, but it then chooses a different way to be seen. That is all death is, you see.

Agnes Whistling Elk
Jaguar Woman

January 28

Where Do I Come From?

See that vanishing point in the center. That is the void. Watch how a path is created by ripples spiraling out from the center. You were born of the void, and the swell is like the outwardness of things. This is like our earthwalk. In our youth and ignorance we walk farther and farther from the center, until we are very far away from our original nature. That is how life is. That is its pattern. Most of us live way out on the perimeter of the spiral. Then, at some point in life, something special happens to you—an insight, a death, and you begin to wonder about yourself and ask questions. "What does life mean? Where do I come from?"

Zoila
Jaguar Woman

January 29

You Are a Sacred Hunter

Always be sure that you're the huntress and not the hunted. The path of the hunter is sacred. Never thoughtlessly kill anything—not even a bug. Imagine if something huge were to flatten you thoughtlessly. Kill only the game you can eat, and don't invade the territory of game that is smarter than you. Always approach your prey with reverence.

Agnes Whistling Elk
Medicine Woman

January 30

See the Awake Ones

You can only be dangerous when you accept your death. Then you become dangerous in spite of anything. You must learn to see the awake ones. A dangerous woman can do anything because she will do anything. A powerful woman will do the unthinkable because the unthinkable belongs to her. Everything belongs to her, and anything is possible. She can track her vision and kill it by making it come true.

Agnes Whistling Elk
Medicine Woman

January 31

Life Is Magical

There is no explaining the world of mystery that surrounds us. All you can know is that life is magical. How that happens is beyond words, beyond explanation, but one day it will also be part of your experience. It is your emotions that keep you from so much of the mysteries in life. Emotions are part of the great beauty in life, and that is the lesson here today. It has to do with movement. You know the teaching of movement. You have experienced that, but you do forget.

Ruby Plenty Chiefs
Shakkai, Woman of the Sacred Garden

February 1

Partake of Your Mother

The source of all power is hidden in our mother, the land. To live we must partake of our mother's body. To engage in sacred study completes the circle. Studying or using the Power Deck, the cards of wisdom, learning more of truth, gives off light. The beings of the earth live in a give and take, a flow of light, that becomes life force and then becomes love. It is law.

Grandmother
The Woman of Wyrrd

February 2

Anything Is Possible

There is more to life than what you see. From where you are standing, anything is possible.

Grandmother
The Woman of Wyrrd

February 3

Respect the Unknown

Great evil has been done on earth by people who think they have all the answers. They have no respect for the unknown. If you do not see all sides of truth and you think that only what you understand is valid, then you dishonor power. You ignore much of the body of the Great Spirit. The body of the Great Spirit is all creation. We are limited as human beings. Most humans live in a tiny little world where only their own perceptions are accepted as real. They will kill for those perceptions. I am asking you to respect what you don't see. Give humble respect to what is unknown and unknowable in the universe.

Ruby Plenty Chiefs
Crystal Woman

February 4

Know Your Barriers

You must know your heyoka barrier. You will become the food of echoes. It is where the east shield is realized. Here you will find the great spirit wheel where sound copies itself. All things are held together by sound, and the slightest noise repeats itself many times. As the water's surface was the first mirror for the eyes, so the heyoka barrier is the first mirror for the ears. But it is more than that, for it helps the opening of your vision eye, the opening to forever. Just as four mirrors can teach you the simple construct of eternity, sound can shatter illusion around the sacred circle and take you there.

Agnes Whistling Elk
Flight of the Seventh Moon

February 5

Live Like an Arrow, Not Like a Target

There are merely two choices in life. You can die frightened or you can live like a worthy huntress and die like one. When your eyes meet those of the greatest huntress, you can say, "I am ready. When the hunt was on, I was valiant. I stalked my prey and killed it appropriately. I was a good provider for my camp, I ate my kill, and I gave it away with respect. I acted on your behalf and represented you well. I realize that I have lived off you, and now I am your meat. We are in agreement. I am ready to go with you to hunt in the spirit world."

Agnes Whistling Elk
Medicine Woman

February 6

Reflection

To balance your dark side with your beauty brings you to power. But remember, it's your own reflection that you're fighting.

Agnes Whistling Elk
Jaguar Woman

February 7

What You Imagine Is Real

"What is behind being able to visualize?"

"Being able to believe in your imagination," I replied.

"That's right. But remember that believing is a tricky concept. A belief structure not only limits your imagining, but also limits your entire consciousness."

Agnes Whistling Elk and Lynn
The Woman of Wyrrd

February 8

Use Your Body-Mind

What is a shaman woman? We are travelers of the dimensions. Do not be caught in the prisms of eternity. Start thinking with your stomach. There are two dogs who stand guard in your stomach. Their names in English are jealousy and fear. One guardian dog is jealously fearful, the other fearfully jealous. They are medicine to protect you.

Agnes Whistling Elk
Medicine Woman

February 9

Understanding

Gaining knowledge of all the ways that people live is a great tool to help you begin to understand that we are here for only a moment, and in the blink of an eye our life will be over.

Grandmother
The Woman of Wyrrd

February 10

Are You Ready for Something Better?

The Star Nations planted wisdom, like seed pods, upon the earth. These seed pods were meant to bloom and bear fruit when the peoples of the earth were ready for higher knowledge.

Agnes Whistling Elk
The Woman of Wyrrd

February 11

The Web of Power

There are many different "muscles" in the body of higher consciousness, and we learn to exercise all of them. If you learn to exercise only the left arm, the right arm becomes weak; it is important to exercise both arms. You understand the physical plane. You are now learning how to dance with the higher energies. You are learning about the subtler bodies. You are learning about the luminous fibers of your being, the web of power. And the web of power can be used in many ways. You can use it to hold you as you cross a great abyss. Your spirit shield grabs onto some of your luminous fibers as it moves out into the universe. That luminous fiber is never let go of—it is attached to the physical body like a silver thread. You can follow it back simply by using your intent.

Grandmother
The Woman of Wyrrd

February 12

Confusion

In transcending the mind, you transcend your confusion. It is the mind that is the troublemaker. It is also the mind that moves you toward power. It is a fine line. Like all things, it is a choice. You can choose your bad habits. You can choose to waste your energy by being muddled and retracing old mistakes, or you can move on into the world of power and take your stand as a woman in this universe.

Shakkai
Shakkai, Woman of the Sacred Garden

February 13

Balance Between Physical and Spiritual Understanding

We stand where two worlds come together, the spiritual and the physical. We are in the womb of our mother, the earth. All things are contained here.

Agnes Whistling Elk
Flight of the Seventh Moon

February 14

Hold, Don't Clutch

Once you take power, you have to keep it. The having is one thing. The holding is another. The feminine part of each of us, male or female, needs to be allowed to operate. Learn to receive, learn to hold. Now I'm not saying clutch. I'm saying hold. A big difference.

Agnes Whistling Elk
Flight of the Seventh Moon

Feeling Guilty

The path of knowledge stings sometimes. It is not an effortless pursuit. Sometimes you get cut, bruised, or even broken. But when you find yourself wounded, that is not the time to feel guilty. It would be inappropriate if I cut off my finger because I sliced it here at the tip. Feeling guilty about your own weakness and failures is as abusive as that. It's like amputating my finger because it's sore and because I've done something stupid like cut myself.

Ruby Plenty Chiefs
Star Woman

February 16

You Are Never Born and You Never Die

Reality does not disappear because of death. Life is eternal. In reality there is no death. What you will be watching is the dismemberment of maya, of the illusion, of the dream that we call life. You know in your heart what dies is only the unreal. Death proves that.

Ani
Windhorse Woman

February 17

Transform Your Body

As we women are related to the water, it is good to be near moving water during your moon. We are born of the first words of the first mother. We are of the void and we carry the void. Our blood is her body. It is sacred. It is said she was born of the water and the earth, and that is why your blood shall return to the earth and your spirit to the waters of the sacred dream. Her power shall be honored over all the earth, and all men shall know her as the beginning. Now that you have transformed your body into the womb time, take care that your blood seed of our first mother is welcomed in a sacred way, for it is of her body.

Agnes Whistling Elk
Flight of the Seventh Moon

February 18

Pray

While you sit here, dream to the Great Mother. Your lap is her altar. Put your essence into your prayers, as we put our blood into her life and ask for balance and understanding in this lifetime. Give of your blood that she may hear you in her dreams and re-member us when she wakes.

Agnes Whistling Elk
Flight of the Seventh Moon

February 19

Attraction

Look again at the spider web. The spider web is very small. It is made by the spider to catch its food. In a sense that is what you do with the fibers within you. You begin to understand as we work that there are things and situations and people that you need in your life, and you can bring them to you. But you do that by making a place within yourself for them to live.

Grandmother
The Woman of Wyrrd

February 20

You Are Magical

Always be receptive to the wilderness of the world—the wilderness of spirit. Allow the mysterious and the strange to become part of your life. Be receptive to the non-ordinary mysteries of life. Many things that we humans need to learn cannot be taught in ordinary ways.

Ani
Windhorse Woman

February 21

Meditate on the Lotus

Meditate on the unity of your body, and visualize the eight-petaled lotus flower. Meditate carefully. Gather your energy and your spirit. Let your mind be at ease. Meditate until you feel the essence of the flower that is truly a reflection of your own essence. See it blooming within your womb. This is the beginning of a long process, so take your time. If it takes a day or a night or an hour, let it happen as it will.

Shakkai
Shakkai, Woman of the Sacred Garden

February 22

See It All

You can understand the effects of the unknowable— you can see Danu rising out of the lake mists at dawn—but you cannot understand how that happens. I can only show you the flames of light around my being, and you can sense the power of that, but I cannot explain it. We call it the arousal of the inner fire. I can lead you there. You can sense the warmth of Danu's smile or feel her wrath as the menacing sea witch. I can help make you strong.

Grandmother
The Woman of Wyrrd

February 23

Are You Coaxing Your Fears?

There are many who coax their fears, and the fears are sure to follow. When you are hunting, one way to call your prey is to find a place in your mind that welcomes him. Your prey will become curious and come and you can have him. Your fears function in the same manner. It is the enemy luring you to your death. Quit coaxing and stay out of sight. Otherwise, you will draw your enemy and it might not go well for you.

Agnes Whistling Elk
Flight of the Seventh Moon

February 24

Rainbows

Watch carefully now, Lynn. A magical being is about to show herself. She is the jeweled mist known as the rainbow. She crosses the world over and has brought us harmony. A rainbow is a great teacher. She has come as a helper. Her spirit presence sought you out, so catch her and learn from her before she vanishes.

Agnes Whistling Elk
Flight of the Seventh Moon

February 25

Gathering Power

There are many roads to walk, many ways, many philosophies, many religions. But the path of the warrioress, the path of the magician or medicine person, is an energy path of the heart. Women move energy out from their center. The first part of their lives is so often spent taking care of family or other people. But a woman, no matter where she is in the world, knows that she does not surrender to this outpouring of energy. She may appear defeated in this male-oriented world, but she is only gathering more power in her humble stance. There is no more fierce warrior than a woman who has learned to change the wind. For if she can change the wind, she has learned to change the direction of her own thoughts, or to still them altogether. This is a quiet, contemplative thing. The circumstances in her life lead her toward her own inward power. The alchemy of moving energy from outer to inner is the alchemy of enlightenment.

Agnes Whistling Elk
Star Woman

February 26

Create a Paradise

You see, in a way I have created my own paradise. What we create in the world, we must first create within ourselves. A long time ago, I realized that we can either live in hell on this earth or we can live in a land of peace and joy, what one might call a paradise. There are really only two ways to live. If one is to find heaven, one has to open one's heart to love. That is the moon gate that one has to walk through to find eternal peace.

Shakkai
Shakkai, Woman of the Sacred Garden

February 27

Lightning

Thoughts and words are like lightning in a storm. Lightning is a gift from the mountain spirits and, like words and thoughts, announces its presence and protection to a new shaman. It is an electrical shock.

Little Green Man to Lynn
Jaguar Woman

February 28

Take Courage

If you are given power, you must know how to keep it. If you steal power, you probably will not have as much trouble keeping it. If you stumble on power and don't take it because of lack of courage, you are not worthy of being a shaman.

Agnes Whistling Elk
Medicine Woman

February 29

Your Presence Transforms Life

When you can talk to a plant, when you know that a plant is alive, has a spirit, you eat the plant and the plant gives away to you. You have the power from the spirit of the plant.

Agnes Whistling Elk
Medicine Woman

March 1

Criticism

It's so easy to criticize, isn't it, Agnes? Because when you criticize, you are simply putting something down that someone else has done, that perhaps you're jealous of, because they've made a commitment, an effort, which you have been unable to do. But to talk constructively about a work of art, something in the world that has been done well, takes creativity. It takes some talent to express that.

Lynn
Shakkai, Woman of the Sacred Garden

March 2

Two Female Energies

There are two kinds of female energy on the earth, not simply one. The earth is female. A woman translates her energy in the form of the ecstatic Rainbow Mother or the nurturing Great Mother.

Zoila
Jaguar Woman

March 3

Those Who Upset You Most Are Your Greatest Teachers

"I serve a different purpose for you. I hang around to feed your fear."

"What do you mean?"

"You see all of your own doubts in me," Ruby said. "You see your anger. You see many things that you don't like, even your own blindness. You don't like to be around me very much because you fear me. There will come a time when you will accept yourself in your totality and you'll become indifferent to me. I will no longer be a threat to you."

Ruby Plenty Chiefs and Lynn
Flight of the Seventh Moon

March 4

Stand Still

Stand within your circle. Turn to face those following you and look them square in the eye.

Agnes Whistling Elk
Flight of the Seventh Moon

March 5

Love Is Nourishment for the Spirit

Remember the nourishment you get from sitting in
the center of your own being, and when you begin
to feel hungry inside for time, for space, you can take
that time, and you will know how to nourish yourself and replenish yourself. Every day the body needs
food and it needs sleep. Your spirit is just the same.
The spirit shield, too, needs to be nourished. For
there to be flames, for you to arouse the inner fire,
there must be something to burn. For there to be
power, there must be life force. So it is important for
you to see how to nourish yourself.

Grandmother
The Woman of Wyrrd

March 6
Who Are You?

Some mirrors have good memory and some don't, just like people. If a mirror remembers you it has something for you to learn. If a mirror doesn't remember you, you better run and find one that does or you may be lost forever. Mirrors are all you have in this earthwalk. If the mirrors forget you, you may as well find a good place to die.

Agnes Whistling Elk
Windhorse Woman

March 7
Knowledge as Wanderer

You have been attracted here as a bee is to a blossom. One of the reasons you are here is to learn. I will teach you. We must siesta now and wait for knowledge. When you are ready to receive her, knowledge will arrive. She is a wanderer but never so far away you cannot entice her into your presence.

Zoila
Jaguar Woman

March 8

What Does Your Fear Look Like?

Fear is part of the unknowable, part of the vast experience we cannot name, for much of our experience as human beings is unnameable. We talk around the feelings. We explain where and how we felt the feelings, but the feeling itself is part of the unknowable. It is something we cannot really touch. The nature of fear is unexplainable, because it is not really there. Fear is elusive and hides from you, but it is not part of the present.

Grandmother
The Woman of Wyrrd

March 9

Have Your Own Identity

Marriage is powerful. Sometimes it can get confused. A man may say, "My wife is a star. I am the pilot. I am producing for her." A woman can destroy a man by her body, language, and thoughts. But in destroying him, she destroys herself. She gives over to his intelligence. She says, "My identity is linked with him, my husband." But her dream should have its own identity. There are many lessons in attachment. But what right do we have to hold on?

Ruby Plenty Chiefs
Flight of the Seventh Moon

March 10

Relax and Trust

Part of what you need to learn in this earthwalk is to relax and trust in the Great Spirit that everything you are doing and feeling is correct for the time.

Agnes Whistling Elk
Shakkai, Woman of the Sacred Garden

March 11

Positive and Negative Poles

Everything begins with a circle of motion. Without positive and negative poles, there would be no movement, no creation. Without the dark side, your beauty would not exist. Don't be afraid to look at both sides. You need them both. You must honor all existence as part of the Great Spirit.

Butterfly Woman
Jaguar Woman

March 12

Every Day Is a Sacred Challenge

"How will I know when I have ripened my void?"

"You will simply become aware of your power. You will feel your time. You cannot avoid it."

"Agnes, I don't understand your terminology. How can I learn all these things?"

"That's why you are here—to learn."

Lynn and Agnes Whistling Elk
Medicine Woman

March 13

Time

Time is only a process of your ego and your mind. Time is a coyote, a trickster. It circles us and keeps us in form in this relative world. It is part of karma; it is part of what we have to let go of, but it should not be let go of until you are truly ready.

Ruby Plenty Chiefs
Shakkai, Woman of the Sacred Garden

March 14

Witness Without Opinion

It is important that you understand this. I do not believe that this god taught right and wrong in the world of nature. What is sacred is sacred, and what is is, and all things that are on this planet are sacred. There is no wrong or right in that sense. There is only God.

Grandmother
The Woman of Wyrrd

March 15

There Is No Returning

Energy always returns to its source when it is born of creativity. In the north, your spirit is inspired with the wisdom of an idea. You take it to the south, to trust and innocence and you dress that inspiration with a physical presence—you manifest your spirit, say, into a book. Then you travel north again for recognition and the fullness of your spirit becomes an exchange of energy with the world. There's a circle there and new energy is born. In throwing out a negative mood or thought, the movement is straight like this stick. You start at one end and drop off the other. There is no returning.

Agnes Whistling Elk
Crystal Woman

March 16

Count on Yourself

With Agnes I could count on nothing. She had warned me: beware of certainty.

Lynn
Flight of the Seventh Moon

March 17

We Are All One

The purpose of sacred work is power. When I tell you you're the black wolf, you look within yourself and you know that you truly are. When you understand the powers of the black wolf, you too will have those powers. All the medicines are good and have power. Your people have this thing that says, "I'm not a snake. I'm not a squirrel. I'm something important." They separate, and that's their tragedy.

Agnes Whistling Elk
Medicine Woman

March 18

Unresolved Thoughts

Every thought you think in your lifetime has a life of its own and has a will to live and survive. This is particularly true when your thoughts are unresolved. Thoughts are like people. They have to be buried properly. If a thought is negative or unresolved, it's lurking around for you to finish what you started and bury it in the right way, make it complete. When your thoughts are contradictory and have no clarity, you create a universe of thought forms that actually live off your energy. And why not? You are their mother in a strange way.

Agnes Whistling Elk
Jaguar Woman

March 19

Simply Listen

"Agnes, you're not going to tell me that rocks make a sound?"

"Yes, I am going to try to describe to you your great unawareness—and how you misinterpret and misunderstand the things around you. Rocks do indeed make a sound. All things that the Great Spirit has put here continually cry to be heard. The problem is, there are few who listen."

Lynn and Agnes Whistling Elk
Flight of the Seventh Moon

SPRING

March 20

Set Aside Time

This is the time when the world changes, the time when you can be transformed. You are the center fire. You are the flowering tree.

Agnes Whistling Elk
Medicine Woman

March 21

Return of the Butterfly

Whenever you see a butterfly, you should feel a gladness in your heart. Yes, the butterfly migrations are ancient spirits returning to the sites of once-great cultures that have now vanished from the earth.

Agnes Whistling Elk
Jaguar Woman

March 22

Life Is a Circle

When you feel the presence of great truth, when you have an opening of light, like an eye seeing something that it has never seen before, it is, perhaps, a glimpse of perfection and beauty. And then the eye closes and that vision is extinguished. You cannot describe that vision, because to describe it exactly is to destroy it, to destroy its power and to lose it. When you describe such a magnificent happening, you must circle it, just as a story that is stalking you circles you. You must describe it in a circular fashion, because all life is a circle, and to reach truth, we must move within that sacred circle. When you move in such a way, you create an atmosphere for truth to live. You create a mirror that people can look into if they choose. Perhaps they will not see exactly the same truth that you saw, but they will find a truth that relates to their own evolving selves.

Ruby Plenty Chiefs
Shakkai, Woman of the Sacred Garden

March 23

Hummingbird Warrior

Watch how the hummingbird hovers in front of the flower. Pollen is power to that tiny bird. She waits until just the right moment and then joins with it. She takes what she needs and flies away.

Zoila
Jaguar Woman

March 24

Seven Sisters

The Great Spirit gave the world a butterfly tree so that the people could learn from it and find joy in its beauty. The tree was filled with colors, and those colors formed rainbows that arched from one camp to another and from one universe to another. The people were united, because they saw the same colors. From this rainbow hung the stars, the moon, the sun, the seven sisters, and the movement of all the heavenly bodies.

Agnes Whistling Elk
Jaguar Woman

March 25

The Stars Live Within You

To shamanize someone, you look at what they can become, not just what they appear to be. Look at the magnificence of possibility in an individual. And then look at what they are, and you locate their pain, their tragedies, their incompleteness. This creates a space between what is and what could be. It is in that void that enlightenment exists. It is from here that we all come and must again return. That is where the stars live within you, the constellations. If you approach a person in the immeasurable void or emptiness and pour your intent into their constellations, you will move them. A shift begins to occur. The stars move and form anew. Pour the intent of your will and the attention of your mind into that place of inward sky, and you initiate their becoming.

Twin Dreamers
Star Woman

March 26

Forget No Part of Yourself

What is forever but a breath of the Great Spirit? The design of the universe is nothing. All of time is but the snap of an arrow in the bow of the Great Spirit. The song of the tribes of plants was sung. The song of the animals was sung. The song of the tribes of man was sung. Every world was remembered in song and no world was forgotten. The Great Spirit is sleeping in all the named and nameless things.

Agnes Whistling Elk
Medicine Woman

March 27

The Sisterhood Is a Circle

The Sisterhood is a circle. It is a circle that lives beyond the limits of time and space. Whether we are incarnate in the physical form or whether we have chosen our death in the physical dimension and have gone on to work in other dimensions, the circle is always the circle. We will never lose each other again.

Agnes Whistling Elk
The Woman of Wyrrd

March 28

The Fate of Controlling

My heart opened until I thought I would burst. My mind was filled with a golden light like the sun. I took a deep breath, and a serenity came upon me as if in the stillness I had frozen my spirit, and all that I had been saying seemed to run like water down through my body and out through my feet into the earth. I saw the face of power, as if for a moment my eyes opened up and saw the truth of what is, that we are all part of each other, that we are, indeed, all one, that there is no death, that it is the mind and the desire and the yearning for wholeness that keeps us from being whole. In that moment of such profound sadness a moment ago, it was as if I let go, finally, because the pain was so deep. I just simply let go. And I realized that to control life is to lose life, that in fact, all that I had thought to be true in the physical world was part of an illusion, a sacred dream, through which we learn.

Lynn
Shakkai, Woman of the Sacred Garden

March 29

Take Your Place

We are all female warriors fighting the war against ignorance. We are trying to reinitiate balance onto the great madre. We have to take our power as women. That doesn't mean become less female. It means to take our place as the goddess, as Xochiquetzal, the goddess of change. She is the mother of us all. We women must be the goddess. Otherwise all is lost.

Zoila
Star Woman

March 30

Dream While Awake

There is another part of you that knows the truth. Learn to dream when you are awake and then you will see what the Great Spirit sees. You will see the windigos, the mythical demons, that are reaching out to you. You will know when you are in danger. You won't have to die a foolish death. You can save yourself and you can save others. They say that the only way to kill a windigo is to melt his heart of ice. Don't be so easily tricked.

Agnes Whistling Elk
Flight of the Seventh Moon

March 31

Suffering

Suffering is like the seed of an herb when planted in the earth. The seed remembers itself and endures in the darkness so that it can grow up into the sunlight one day as an entirely transformed flower. When you understand the suffering and the forces of darkness, you can end suffering and bring light to the people.

Ginevee
Crystal Woman

Where Is Your Center?

Nothing stands without reason. You can develop your awareness by examining anything closely. Looked at properly, an object will cry out to you. When you know enough, you will see much about a person by the way she picks up a glass or pencil. You can see a thousand things in action. You can know all about a hunter by the way he builds a fire, just as you can know about a bird by the way it builds its nest. When you look at an object, you can see how much of a center it has. A true power object has a center. You are drawn to these things, and you don't even know why.

Agnes Whistling Elk
Medicine Woman

April 2

Still Point Within the Magician

When you look out at the world and you see the activity of all human beings, when you see their movement, their spiritual and physical activity, you realize that at the center of all that pandemonium there is a still point, and the still point is within the magician. The still point is the point of creation, the place where true power lives.

Grandmother
The Woman of Wyrrd

April 3

Trust and Faith Are Two Halves of Your Self Shield

Trusting what comes is part of loving. It is your trust that builds the bridge between this physical dream we live in and the dream of your spirit. In a sense that is what love is made of—the totality of mind and soul. The bridge or connection, then, is trust.

Agnes Whistling Elk
The Woman of Wyrrd

April 4

The Confines of Language

When you speak of truth, when you speak of the beauties of wisdom and knowledge, it is very difficult to contain that knowledge within the confines of a word or two, or a sentence, because each word, each innuendo of sound, means something different to each person who speaks it and who hears it. We are talking about communication, in a sense, with the Tao, with our creator. To manifest a truth into the world is sometimes better done through art. You can express through art the subtleties of form and color and brush stroke. A stone placed a certain way in a garden stimulates a sense of knowing that is indescribable, that is beyond the spoken word. It is like poetry. The real truth of poetry is between the words, between the lines.

Shakkai
Shakkai, Woman of the Sacred Garden

April 5

The Great Spirit Is a Quality of Being

People have denied the possibilities of magic, the light that is real even though it cannot be touched. The strange dimensions of life happen just as much as scientific discoveries. In actuality "black hole" discoveries are the beginning of proof of the strange and magical dimensions of our existence. "Strange" usually means only that it is something that occurs out of our frame of reference, out of our realm of experience. "Strange magic" means beyond our understanding or the limits of our mind, something that is weird and bad. Mind is like this rice bowl, and rice is our knowledge. The rice is limited by the confines of this bowl. Be a magician and stay open to the mysteries. Let your wisdom reach beyond the limits of ordinary mind. Life, existence, is a mystery. Symbolically, your knowledge is not limited to a simple rice bowl, and that is the way it will always be. Instead of fighting for the rice bowl, fight to make beautiful rice.

Ani
Windhorse Woman

April 6

Fear of Death

You're scared because you've lost control. When a child grows up minding her parents and is always afraid of their reactions to things, she learns to control her environment to survive. Control in those terms means being able to live. Whenever you are taken off guard you feel like you have lost control. The root of all fears is the same. It is fear of death. When you lose control you think you will die.

Ruby Plenty Chiefs
Crystal Woman

April 7

Wildness

We were all born wild like a mountain lion, and to live in civilization we become sheep at a very young age. We become tame. But we are not house pets. We are fierce and wild by nature. Movement between one life situation and another is essential.

Movement or action is the key that unlocks the door to understanding. Dream on this. Consider what is left of your instinctual nature. Remember that action is not a reaction. It has a lodge of its own. When you see a horse, you become both happy and sad. That horse represents the wildness within yourself that you have never dared to become.

Twin Dreamers
Star Woman

April 8

Use All of Your Senses

Shaman power is the power to bring harmony and balance into your life and into the life of others. When you begin to balance yourself in a shaman way, you begin to see magical glimpses because you are telling the beings of the earth that you believe in beauty. As a storyteller you must understand this. You are becoming a woman spinner. To learn about power is to spin or to weave the concept of life into tangible forms. To lift beyond your ordinary vision and see the forces that give us life. This is why I am teaching you to understand things with all of your being, with all of your senses. Your sight, hearing, taste, smell—all that you are as woman.

Agnes Whistling Elk
Flight of the Seventh Moon

April 9

Paddling Upstream

A heavy mist was moving through the pines and settled down over us. The experience was dreamlike, the mist first clearing and then sweeping around us in the canoe. Shafts of sunlight burst through the greyness. The water had calmed and was like oiled slate. The sound of our paddles was muffled and rhythmic. Soon we were pulling upstream on the river.

I giggled to myself.

"What are you laughing at?" Agnes asked.

"I was just thinking," I said. "This is a real good metaphor for my life—paddling upstream in a fog."

"I heard a better one, only it was without a paddle," Agnes said.

"That too," I agreed, laughing heartily.

Agnes Whistling Elk and Lynn
Flight of the Seventh Moon

April 10

Observe Your Feelings

Fear gives you a perfect opportunity to learn. It gives you the opportunity to witness, and when I say witness, I mean just to sit very silently and watch, not meditate, but just observe your feelings as they well up inside you, your feelings of pain, of whatever comes up. You need just to witness; watch what happens; do not make any movement or any judgment or choice. Just simply watch what happens. The witnessing will nourish the brilliance inside you.

Grandmother
The Woman of Wyrrd

April 11

Warrior of the Spirit

When you want to control another person, you do not love that person. Not only do you not love them, but you become incapable of loving, because controlling is a restriction, a constriction. Loving is an opening and a letting go. When you let go to the magic that is around you and allow yourself to be open to love, then ecstasy is possible, because then you step into the world of the unknown, where there is no control. Then you step into the void where magic lives, where power lives. You become a true warrior of spirit.

Shakkai
Shakkai, Woman of the Sacred Garden

April 12

We Are Afraid to Give Up What We Know, Even If It Hurts

People are afraid to become wise. Human beings are afraid to try anything new. It is the tragedy of human life, as we have spoken about before. Even though something new may make us feel better, we are still afraid.

Grandmother
The Woman of Wyrrd

April 13

Unconditional Love

"One day, Little Wolf, you will understand that to be loved, it is not necessary to accomplish. It is only necessary to be, simply to exist in your state of awareness. If you want to accomplish something out of that state, that is fine, and if you do not, that is fine too. There is unconditional love in the universe, not only from your friends and teachers; certainly we love you, but somehow there are times when you don't feel that."

"Yes, that is true, Ruby. Sometimes I feel very alone, very isolated and separated from everyone and everything. And there are other times when I feel at the center of the universe. I know that I am one with the Great Spirit."

"But you see," Ruby said, "those changes are very important. Those shifts, those movements, are important. Remember, enlightenment is within the process and contained in the process of movement. Without that movement, there is no life."

Ruby Plenty Chiefs and Lynn
Shakkai, Woman of the Sacred Garden

April 14

Enjoy Your Opportunities

Remember that we choose to come onto this earth to become enlightened. This physical body provides a great opportunity. When we are in the dimension of Spirit, it is obvious that the physical dimension can give us a chance to erect and choose mirrors through family work and life situations. It is with these mirrors that enlightenment becomes possible.

Ani
Windhorse Woman

April 15

An Agreement with Time

Mind and time are all within the self lodge circle. Space and our relatedness to all life is also within the self lodge circle. In your language the self lodge is the ego. The ego is an entity that exists by way of an agreement between time, mind, and space. Without that agreement you would not have an ego. Without that agreement you would be outside of what you would call relativity or the time-space continuum. We talked long ago about your scientist Einstein. He was close to a great truth in his mind that shamans have always known with their bodies. We shamans have always known how to trick time. If you take any of those agreements out of the self lodge circle, you alter your relatedness to all living things. It is an essential part of the process of healing. Each agreement between time, space, and mind adds up to ego.

Agnes Whistling Elk
Crystal Woman

April 16

Don't Invite Negativity into Your Life

I learned that our fear creates our own negativity. Negativity from other people as a thought form can certainly come into any field, but it's not going to harm me unless I allow it to. I can send it back to the person who sent it to me.

Lynn
The Woman of Wyrrd

April 17

What Is Your Lesson in This Lifetime?

Your spirit knows no limits. There are no boundaries to your being. You are part of infinity. In the physical aspect of your life, you are limited. You have commitments. There are rules that restrict you. You are a woman in a man's world, and you must do certain things, but you have chosen to be born into the world at this time for a reason. There must be things that you need to learn about the world that exists today. The more constricted your life is on a physical plane, the more you are going to want to break free of those boundaries and give wings to your being in spirit flight.

Grandmother
The Woman of Wyrrd

April 18

Experience Your Femaleness

We live in a time of vision, a time when the people of
Mother Earth are eager for a new and more balanced
way of life. First we must heal the body of Mother
Earth with a renewed understanding of feminine
consciousness. We must move out into the world to
experience what is missing. What is missing is an understanding and incorporation of the primal woman.

Agnes Whistling Elk
Windhorse Woman

April 19

We Are Food

We are each the food for our brothers and sisters.
Whether we are hungry wolves, fish, or the wind,
we all devour one another and become transformed.
Your problem is that you get caught in believing the
dream. You get too close to what you are looking at,
and you miss the greater vision. You forget the
dreamer. There is a warrior trout out there in the

river who has spent his whole life preparing for this combat. It's his destiny and yours. When you meet your trout, honor the power of that moment and give way to the magnitude of your destiny with him.

Ruby Plenty Chiefs
Star Woman

April 20

Yield

Those two-chief dreams are great luck. You had to trick power to find it. Its symbol is big medicine, medicine that woman has forgotten. It was greatly dangerous, but now you can help them remember that medicine. You have smoked the male and female within your lodge-self and you have come to a place where the roads fork. You can change and grow. You begin to understand what it really means to yield. Woman thinks she yields, but she has forgotten how. Many women's lodges stand deserted because no one looks inside. Reach out for that high warrior waiting in the woman's lodge. Embrace him and be free.

Agnes Whistling Elk
Medicine Woman

April 21

Giveaway

The meat that you are eating now, that is your sister. We eat our brothers and sisters. You're a cannibal. Your sister has fallen down so that you may have life.

Agnes Whistling Elk
Medicine Woman

April 22

Earthwalk

We are escaping our delusions. There are other ways of seeing. All of life is a trail that leads to the Great Tree or the Great Spirit. Everyone is on this path. Some are, for the moment, lost. Some are resting. Some realize the truth but can go no further.

Agnes Whistling Elk
Jaguar Woman

You Are a Gift from the First Mother's Heart

The flesh of the first mother has been burned that you may be given life. Her smoke will bring wisdom to your way. Smoke is a gift from the first mother's heart. Bless her memory, for she lives within you. When you eat, it is she who eats. When you smoke, it is she who takes your message to the faraway. When you bleed, it is she who bleeds. When you give your body to be divided in love, let all parts of you be in her name so that her love can be complete on this great earth.

Agnes Whistling Elk
Flight of the Seventh Moon

April 24

Shields

I unwrapped my four shields and placed them in their four directions around me. I was proud as I did this. I concentrated on the symbolism that I had put into each shield. My dreams and visions were an aspect of the very form and fabric of which they were built. The shields stood for the concept of who I am in my completeness. Together, they were the ultimate medicine wheel, the map from my outer to my inner being. To conceive of them was to conceive the mystery of my oneness.

Lynn
Flight of the Seventh Moon

April 25

Addictions

When you are not a warrioress, when you do not face the world lightly, there are many pitfalls, the pitfalls of addictions. When you fall into one of your addictions, let's say sadness, what you are really doing is bleeding off your precious life force. And that ice cube that you are just becomes colder. In this process of staying cold, and feeling not a sense of oneness but a state of being in duality, you are separate from the sea of the Great Spirit. There is no opening of the great mirror. There is no transcendence. The warrioress must face herself in the great mirror to heat up, to melt.

Agnes Whistling Elk
Star Woman

April 26

Be a Queen, Not a Princess

Women are like sponges. You can squeeze them until there is nothing left of them, squeeze all the life out of them, the water, and let go of the sponge, the woman, and she goes right back to her original shape to go on with life. A woman has extraordinary endurance. There is a special power within a woman because she understands the true energy of Mother Earth. There is indeed a reason why Mother Earth has been called female.

Lynn
Windhorse Woman

April 27

Fear Can Help You

The beings of light, the great spirit circle of sisters, can be frightening. When the sisters come to meet with you, it is the very fact that they frighten you that they heal you. They see your fear. They see the fabric and the design of the webs within you, and they move into that energy field, and they loosen the fibers. To do that, they must work within your own fear. It is your fear, for once, that can help you.

Grandmother
The Woman of Wyrrd

April 28

Vulnerability

Only if you have ego is there a conflict between the dark and the light. If there is no ego, there is no fight. There is only a divine vulnerability, which is your very best shield and defense.

Shakkai
Shakkai, Woman of the Sacred Garden

April 29

The Mother Stars

You think that your life has nothing to do with any other life. This is the self-council. In self-council you must separate and become responsible for your own power. This process cuts cords that bleed your much-needed energy. When that is accomplished, a realization occurs. You open to the grand council and the great council fires within. You begin to understand that the galaxies, the mother stars, all existence, in fact, awakens within your own being. In a sense you are all existence. You are the womb from which the stars are born. All life is your firstborn child. The trees, the flowers, and all the creatures of earth have their rootedness in your special being. It does not seem so, but it has always been that way. To know these things, the central council fires of your personal experience must be ignited, and you must warm your hands on your own inner-spirit flame.

Agnes Whistling Elk
Star Woman

April 30

The Backward Way

Heyoka is an awake one. They walk backward because they know God is behind them. Trust and fall backward—they know the Great Spirit will catch them. They make you see yourself and your illusions. They dance the peace dance in a time of war.

Ruby Plenty Chiefs
Flight of the Seventh Moon

May 1

New Vision

There is an illumination of higher knowledge. The true answer, that which illuminates us, is within. It illuminates in a new way even that which is clearly seen.

Agnes Whistling Elk
Jaguar Woman

May 2

You Are the Still Point of a Storm

Now Ruby is blind but she sees more than anyone. Four Deer led her to the center of this outwardly violent circle and taught her how to quiet herself. She will always see because she is always in that center.

Agnes Whistling Elk
Medicine Woman

May 3

See the Beauty in All Things

I've told you many times that there is nothing without reason. There is justice—maybe not immediately, but the Great Spirit has forever to work it out. We humans just have this brief span until we fall down. I want to spend my days as a warrioress and recognize the beauty in all things. An animal is a child of the universe, like you and me. Taking the life of a wild and free animal should be done with the understanding of your own death. Otherwise, leave it be.

Agnes Whistling Elk
Medicine Woman

May 4

Masks

Masks have the power to transform. If you meet a person who is truly deceptive, there should be a mask somewhere he could put on that would be what he really is.

Agnes Whistling Elk
Flight of the Seventh Moon

May 5

You Are a Stealthy Being

Stealthy beings can be any place at any time, and you can wait for a stealthy being forever and never see one. Only a stealthy being can see another stealthy being. A stealthy being has dreams that are real.

Agnes Whistling Elk
Medicine Woman

May 6

Heal All Life

All living things eat other living things to survive. That is life, that is the nature of our dream. You are made of other life-forms. You take spirit power from those life-forms and you are made into an extraordinary being that is comprised of parts of all living things. You experience all life and then you can heal all life as it heals you.

Agnes Whistling Elk
Crystal Woman

May 7

The First Mirror

Imagine you're leaning over a pool of water—the first mirror. You dive into the water and your reflection comes up to meet you. What happens to your reflection on the plane of the surface of the pool? You can see that's a kind of crossroads—if you can unravel that, you can go beyond the crossroads. It's just another symbol. Going beyond what's known into the unknown. You have true death in enlightenment—this is one of many mysteries. The end is where seven roads fork the dream. Choose one of the roads if you want power, or you can run back and say, "I've gone too far."

Ruby Plenty Chiefs
Flight of the Seventh Moon

May 8

What Is Your Tone?

The eyes have a closer kinship with the ears than you realize. Your eyes echo and this causes vision. Every object, every plant, animal, and human has a distinct sound. I have told you that Ruby is the Keeper-of-the-Face-of-the-Shields. Each shield has a unique face, as each human has a unique face. Each face makes a unique noise.

Agnes Whistling Elk
Flight of the Seventh Moon

May 9

Wake Up the Spirits

Beautiful music wakes up the spirits. They sleep and wait for us to come and entice them to awaken. That's why I sing and say beautiful things to my spirits.

Zoila
Jaguar Woman

May 10

Center, Ease, and Joy

One of the great teachings of this particular time in history is to learn how to live one's life with the stress of three or four lives all at once and still maintain your center and your ease and your joy—a very, very difficult thing to do. But it is like a problem in logic, like a mathematical equation using trade beads. It can be done, but the right symbolism has to be learned. The right thoughts must be written for the outcome to be beautiful.

Agnes Whistling Elk
Shakkai, Woman of the Sacred Garden

May 11

Finding Your Way Home

All there is, is the pure beauty of truth. It is the truth that we are in fact all one, that the duality of this life is simply an illusion. What is all of this wisdom and all of this work and all of this struggle but the Great Spirit creating a way for us to find our way home? You are walking down the trail toward home. Never forget that.

Agnes Whistling Elk
The Woman of Wyrrd

May 12

Be Dangerous

You are not a dangerous woman. You are like a clipped bird in some ways—beating your wings without purpose. I see a woman who needs much more will and courage—true courage. You are not at all as simple as you look. The saddest thing I see is that you like to think you're important. For me, I prefer being important to fooling myself.

Agnes Whistling Elk
Medicine Woman

May 13

Witness Everything

In this life—you are really dreaming. You may be dreaming of a beautiful heaven or the darkest hell, but a dream it is. When you awake into death you are left naked. You are naked of all that you have collected. You have lost all that you have aspired to do.

Ani
Windhorse Woman

May 14

Go Beyond Thought

The rainbow comes to teach you about thought. A rainbow appears to be a connecting link from one point to another point. The same is true of thought. She has no beginning and no ending. This is also true of thought. You can't catch hold of a rainbow; you can't catch hold of thought. She may be weak or strong, clear or unclear. The same is true of thought. She makes something where there is a semblance of nothing. So does thought. She is colored by the sun, the sky, the wind, as thought is colored by emotion. For some it is more difficult to go beyond thought than it is to go beyond this beautiful rainbow child.

Agnes Whistling Elk
Flight of the Seventh Moon

May 15

Be a Woman of Ability

You must learn to be a woman of ability. You must make a decision to learn to help yourself. You must learn to make star shields. To make a shield in the proper manner, you have to destroy conflicting parts of yourself.

Agnes Whistling Elk
Flight of the Seventh Moon

May 16

Know Your Form

Women need a form that is a counterpart of the male form, but one that is truly their own. In emulating men, women give up their power, their specialness.

Agnes Whistling Elk
Flight of the Seventh Moon

May 17

Master Your Destiny

Continue to use your intuition—you can never solve a problem on the level at which it is born. To steal the marriage basket you have to be relentless in your pursuit. Be the master of your destiny, because you have the necessity to manifest yourself.

Agnes Whistling Elk
Medicine Woman

May 18

Sacred Witness

You must stay centered, always living in your center, looking out from that place of your sacred witness into the world.

Agnes Whistling Elk
Shakkai, Woman of the Sacred Garden

May 19

Bigger Vision

To limit yourself to one set of beliefs, to limit your wisdom to what is known in one time and place, is pure ignorance. There are many times and many places.

Grandmother
The Woman of Wyrrd

May 20

Explore the Vast Dimensions of Life

You must remember that when you move out of this physical, dualistic existence, you are moving away from the reference of the time-space relativity that we experience here. We are moving out of time. That is why, when you are working in the astral, it is impossible to tell what time it is. What you are doing when you dreamwalk is moving into history, into the past. You are exploring your lifetime.

Agnes Whistling Elk
The Woman of Wyrrd

May 21

Seek Your Vision

There are many roads to power. Power is gained primarily from visions and dreams, but now I hope it makes sense to you that it is also honorable to take power.

Agnes Whistling Elk
Medicine Woman

May 22

Feel the Power

Those are the water babies that haven't been born yet. They're inside you, always crying. They represent your unborn powers. They have been crying for a thousand years, where the wheels of mystery spin forever. Take the trust of those crying children. Feel the power in yourself of woman, of mother. You are the very Mother Earth itself.

Agnes Whistling Elk
Medicine Woman

May 23

You're on Your Way Home

All trails lead back to the center—all spirit. All ways, all religions, lead back to the center. Walk within goodness.

Agnes Whistling Elk
Medicine Woman

May 24

Intent

Any woman can belong to the Sisterhood, Lynn. Many spend their lifetime in search of us and never find anything but their own meandering trail. Others come into our midst without the slightest effort, because their hearts are true.

Agnes Whistling Elk
Jaguar Woman

May 25

Trust

There are always helpers and signs to point the way for anyone who is willing to follow them. Unknowingly, for the first time in your life, you have followed your true path.

Agnes Whistling Elk
Flight of the Seventh Moon

May 26

Conquer Your Fear

When you have let loose of your fears to let them flutter off on their own accord, you will remember that the ancient way of strength is feminine, of the womb. It is receptive. You can hold up the shields and become self-reliant. When you become indifferent to me, your fear will have flown away. That will be a big power time for you.

Ruby Plenty Chiefs
Flight of the Seventh Moon

May 27

You Are Made of Love

You can live more fully in your heart. Love is the bridge you have built with faith. Now you must have the trust to walk across the abyss of a vast darkness. That bridge is love, and it forms the connection between your body and your spirit.

Ruby Plenty Chiefs
The Woman of Wyrrd

May 28

Another Flowering

There is a barrier, an invincible barrier between the physical world and the next world that we are born into at death. Life is beautiful in so many aspects, and death is merely a passageway to the next state of beauty, another blossom, another flowering. We have only three dimensions in this physical world that we call life. When we move on to the other side, we have more to experience. We have a fourth hoop of power. We are moving into four dimensions. Our awareness, our vision, our ability to perceive truth and God, the sacred Tao, is expanded beyond your imagination.

Shakkai
Shakkai, Woman of the Sacred Garden

May 29

See with the Eyes of a Shamaness

We are in the passageway to the great dream. It is here when you descend that you are born, and it is here that when you ascend the cord is cut, and you are separated from your mother. But she will be reborn in you. You are her place of becoming, and we are in the lair of eternal return. Here you are going to learn to see what is hidden—to see with the eyes of a shamaness.

Agnes Whistling Elk
Flight of the Seventh Moon

May 30

See Through to the End

"What happens when a person dies, Agnes?"

"It's not an important question. The whole of a human's life is watched by the thunder chiefs. You have a road within you, a turquoise road. The important thing is to keep your spirit moving along this road. If you do that, in the end of your days you will merge with the thunder chiefs. All your other roads lead back into absurdity and delusion. Those roads swell with pain, sorrow, and confusion. I have a little power because I see through to the end. In the end, all the riddles are solved and the paradoxes are answered. In the end, the meaning of your tears and suffering is clear. And if you find it in your time, you will be full and no one can take it away from you. That is the shaman's way and, for you, that is the right way."

Lynn and Agnes Whistling Elk
Medicine Woman

May 31

A Test of Wills

You have been through a test of wills. You have moved through a darkness like the shadows that surround a dying person. You had to move through the darkness of your pain alone, so that you could emerge on the other side through the effort of your own individual will. From your extraordinary isolation of will, you feel the first taste of true achievement. This achievement looks like understanding, like a knowing in the silence of the night, but the day of wisdom will come and the sun will rise, and there is a meaning to all the pain and to all the joy.

Agnes Whistling Elk
Shakkai, Woman of the Sacred Garden

June 1

Make an Act of Beauty

You are always faced with choices. You have the choice to nourish or you have the choice to destroy with your power. When you teach apprentices about power, it is very important to take them through their fears in the beginning, because evil and manipulation are caused by greed and envy, which are born of fear. To go through your own fears, you have to learn of yourself. It is hard to know of yourself without making an act of power or an act of beauty.

Agnes Whistling Elk
Flight of the Seventh Moon

June 2

Trust Yourself

We are the only ones who can heal ourselves—sometimes with assistance, sometimes not. Trust yourself. Listen to your own voice.

Agnes Whistling Elk
Jaguar Woman

June 3

Beauty

Beauty always has another side. If you look at something carefully, as a shamaness, you will always be able to see the dark side too. One cannot exist without the other and yet, people choose never to look into the shadows.

Butterfly Woman
Jaguar Woman

June 4

Witness What You Believe In

Those rocks represent each of your beliefs. There is the hoop of the world and the hoop of the self. Your hoops are like nests that surround you—very comforting. But you must recognize the existence of such safe nests. You must see that you sit on those rocks as if they were eggs and you were the mother hatching them. You must see that you are not free because you will never leave your nest of self-ignorance. You can spend the rest of your life hatching that if you want to. Those eggs will be the boundaries of your experience.

Agnes Whistling Elk
Medicine Woman

June 5

You Are Already Home

We're like that mountain. The extent of her power and beauty is hidden from view; at the top she is lost in a dream. Before we are born onto this earthwalk, we wait for a great blessing—our chance to be born onto earth. We know that we come here to be enlightened. When we are born, the dream begins. Like the cloud hiding the mountaintop, the dream obscures our true vision. We must gather a strong wind to blow away the clouds. Then we can see, truly see, the whole of our being—the silent mountain that we are. That is what life is all about: waking up from the dream. We have come here to become enlightened, yet it is the one thing that we are most afraid of.

Agnes Whistling Elk
The Woman of Wyrrd

June 6

Shed Old Baggage Like a Snake Shedding Skin

I felt a special tenderness for her. Her face was a messenger of great pain to me, because it reminded me that what I had known as my life was dying. I couldn't even explain to myself how I was different, but I knew I was evolving into a person I wouldn't have recognized a few months ago. It was like being in love.

Lynn, writing about Agnes
Medicine Woman

June 7

Pray for All That Lives

There is spirit in all things. There is spirit in the rocks, in the trees, in the earth, in people and animals, and in our wondrous flying friends.

Grandmother
The Woman of Wyrrd

June 8

Think with Your Body-Mind

The way of Wyrrd is about power. It is about under-standing energy and the flow of energy, seeing the many faces of the Mother Goddess. From the begin-ning of time there have been certain gifted people who have understood life and its flows, and they gave it a name. They called it energy, but they could not explain what it was. They just know that they felt it, and they knew that they could use it to heal.

Grandmother
The Woman of Wyrrd

June 9

Hummingbird

The hummingbird is a great warrior. He can lead you to the food that you need to live. Watch him and study his ways.

José
Jaguar Woman

June 10

Other Levels of Power

Now you must learn a new lesson. There is such a thing as awareness. We talk of it often. We use the word easily. But we do not understand the importance of awareness on a level other than physical reality. To become aware of your luminous fibers and their strength and power in other dimensions is to become aware on many levels. You are strengthening your awareness in the other circles of power besides this one.

Ruby Plenty Chiefs
The Woman of Wyrrd

June 11

Food for Spirit

When a woman of power looks at you she sees what's going on. Most people invite the guests and furnish themselves as the meal. Fears always manifest themselves to the one who creates them. I can see when your spirit is food and what entity is eating you. You have many fears around you, and that is why you are so heavy. Without your food-gift of energy, the entity would waste away and perish.

Agnes Whistling Elk
Jaguar Woman

June 12

Excuses

There are no excuses for anything. You change things or you don't. Excuses rob you of power and induce apathy.

Agnes Whistling Elk
Jaguar Woman

June 13

Ego

There are plateaus of learning in the life of every apprentice. When you reach the top of the mountain, you have to descend in order to climb the next mountain on your journey. Many times you will think your journey is over when you reach the top of the mountain. Do not be fooled. These are moments of great deception, like a bird flying against the window. You can sit on the mountain forever, saying, "This is who I am. I am a writer. I am a teacher. I am a shaman woman." Don't you see you are sitting on your own ego?

Agnes Whistling Elk
Flight of the Seventh Moon

June 14

Clinging to Addictions

"Haven't you wondered why it is difficult to find your true nature?"

"Yes, I have tried to find my way home."

"Go back to the source. Watch the whirlpool. From such powers the universe has evolved. The powers of the universe are within you. See how everything is swallowed into the center? It is ordained that all be pulled in. The universe will feed into itself, and all creatures great and small will be liberated."

"Then why is it so difficult for us, Zoila?"

"Because of ignorance and false identity. Perhaps it is identification with objects and clinging to addictions that keep you from the source."

Zoila and Lynn
Jaguar Woman

June 15

Train Your Spirit Shield

The life force comes down from the Old One and infuses the physical body with life when a person is born onto this Mother Earth. It is after the person is born that the spirit shield is activated. The spirit shield that you have experienced shining through your luminous fibers is part of this lifetime and can move around in all dimensions if it is trained. When you die the spirit shield goes into the earth. When you die the life force goes back into the Old One. Occasionally, if someone is trained properly, the spirit shield can move on, as it is in this lifetime, to another lifetime.

Grandmother
The Woman of Wyrrd

June 16

It Is Good to Have a Dream

Your life is a path. Knowingly or unknowingly you have been on a vision quest. It is good to have a vision, a dream.

Agnes Whistling Elk
Medicine Woman

June 17

All That I Love

I love nature, and I realized that nature represents the goodness of the human spirit, a perfection of the Tao that is within each of us. So what is better than to spend my life meditating on nature, meditating on a beautiful flower until the fragrance of that flower becomes part of my own spirit? You see, all that we love is here. The sacred mountains and the spirits of the mountains are represented here in my garden with the stones, and we can see the reflection of our mountain in the water beside us. All I need is to move out of my house and sit here and meditate with the most high. What could be better?

Shakkai
Shakkai, Woman of the Sacred Garden

June 18

Expand Your Heart

There is nothing you do that does not strengthen your spirit. That is what this life is all about—to evolve. So everything you do is an exercise, in a way, to bring you closer to the Great Spirit.

Agnes Whistling Elk
The Woman of Wyrrd

June 19

Sacred Form

We make such a drama out of life. For some reason the human being has to develop an extraordinary ego just to exist. Because of that ego, we think we are better than the flowers, better than the animals and the birds, and certainly better than other human beings and races that are not our own, but in fact life is simply life, and life is sacred. Beyond anything, life is sacred. There is a sacred form to everything.

Agnes Whistling Elk
Shakkai, Woman of the Sacred Garden

June 20

Darkness Defines the Light

Light comes from the sun. You cannot touch it. Does that mean it is not real?

Ani
Windhorse Woman

SUMMER

June 21

Light in the Bamboo

Through all the veils of ignorance, the truth and goodness of life and nature will survive. With each act of power that you perform, the light on earth is increased a tiny, tiny bit. It is like looking to the bamboo and seeing the morning light reflecting off the pond. It brings you closer to home.

Ruby Plenty Chiefs
Shakkai, Woman of the Sacred Garden

June 22

The Lessons of Power

The first lesson of power is that we are all alone. We think we are our bodies. We think we are our belief structures, our minds, our egos. We think we are what we do in the world, but that is an illusion. So the last lesson of power is that we are really all one. Whatever we're doing out there is part of our learning process. But inside us is this magnificent light. It is the reflection of the sacred Tao. That is the same essence of the mountain, the sacred mountain, that lives within us and within which we live.

Shakkai
Shakkai, Woman of the Sacred Garden

June 23

Illumination

I looked at Agnes and suddenly realized that knowledge is a kind of wall that has to be torn down in order to experience illumination. I saw the great simplicity of it all and I laughed. I had turned a difficult corner on my path, and I laughed all that day and the next day as well. It was so obvious and yet so elusive. Each time the realization came back to me, I laughed out loud. A teacher keeps you from the very thing you are looking for. And what is truth? asked Pontius Pilate, washing his hands.

Lynn
Flight of the Seventh Moon

June 24

I Am Full

My tears are of joy. It is the joy of communication, of knowing that finally, through our work with you, you are beginning to see, to truly see, what we are all about. It is a great joy to me because, as you know in your own life, when you work in the world of power as a woman of power, you make a few dear friends and isolate yourself from the world, because very few can understand your commitment, your pain, your desire for compassion and love. Few can relate to your life and what you seek. When I look at you, I see a woman who understands my heart, and that makes me very full.

Ruby Plenty Chiefs
Shakkai, Woman of the Sacred Garden

U

Old Holy One

Do you know why we teach you about miniature gardens? When we are of the world, we are prey to anyone who sees us. Everyone wants the great people, the masters, the great minds of our time. They move into the world and they are often destroyed. People want what they have, because they shine so brightly. Everyone is attracted to them and can see them. Hidden in the mountains are beautiful ones and sacred ones, but because they do not hide well enough, they are hunted and destroyed. Jade is hidden within a rock. It is not enough that its beauty be left there. The rock must be smashed and the jade revealed and polished. This is not because we want to harm the rock, but because we want the jade for its beauty and value. So I say to you, the better you hide, the better you will be protected. If you hide behind the mountain screens, you will not be seen. You will not be killed. That is why, when there is great wisdom in the world, its beauty shines and everybody sees it, and then the world will take it for their

U

own use. So the great sisterhoods and brotherhoods recall the knowledge and the wisdom. They reveal this knowledge and wisdom through the rocks, trees, and sacred springs, and perhaps through a gnarled and crippled old woman.

The Old Holy One
Shakkai, Woman of the Sacred Garden

June 26

Invisible Places

The squirrel is very wise. Two-leggeds have learned from him over the centuries. He knows the turn of the season wheels and he collects food and prepares for winter. The squirrel knows many things about food that humans have yet to learn. They're familiar with tree spirits and tree magic. They know secret places of power, places that radiate with enough energy to drive the human crazy. They know of invisible places and will bring the love of one tree for another.

Agnes Whistling Elk
Flight of the Seventh Moon

June 27

New Worlds Are Being Born

The road to self-realization is steep and treacherous. You may react and become scared because you sense your vulnerability. You may talk constantly and become angry, but few initiates will listen and realize that new worlds are being born.

Twin Dreamers
Star Woman

June 28

Be All That You Are

Love is a good guide. Knowledge is a good guide. Sharing is a good guide. Self-teaching is a good guide. I do not have to believe to know sorrow—I know when I sorrow. I don't have to believe to know love—I know when I love. I don't have to believe to have joy—I know when I am joyful. To be here I am here. So do not believe that you are only human. Know yourself. There are many medicines.

Agnes Whistling Elk
Medicine Woman

June 29

Luminous Fibers

You and I and all people, all beings that are alive on this earth, are standing on an enormous tapestry called life, and that tapestry is made of fibers. They are luminous, and on some level they shine like the sun. You are beginning to walk differently. You are beginning to see the spirit shields, and you are beginning to understand a little about life force. All these things, one and another, are part of each other.

Grandmother
The Woman of Wyrrd

June 30

Shaman Death

Remember the sacred spiral. At the center is the formless unknowable. The center represents your shaman death where you finally let go of the lodges of the mind and ego and our relative sense of time. On the perimeter of the spiral is our form and our lodges of earthly endeavor. When I talk to you about

U

enlightenment and merging with the centers of the sacred spiral, your mind becomes frightened. Your mind understands only the concept of enlightenment and loss of form. But we have enthroned the mind as king of our lives and it is really only a tool like your hand. When you speak of a shaman death or form-lessness, the mind thinks it's going to die. There is also a keeper of the mind. She would rather see you go crazy and develop many addictions than become a formless shaman. The mind, in its confusion, thinks that's the only way it will survive as a mind.

Ruby Plenty Chiefs
Crystal Woman

July 1

Support One Another

Agnes began to backpaddle. She said, "Have you ever noticed how much faster we can go when we paddle together? Look what happens to the canoe when I work against you." We started to pitch and tip dangerously. "In your society, women get together in little groups and fight against each other instead of giving one another power and direction. It is a great tragedy for the world that your women don't have clans and traditions. With the support of other women you can do practically anything."

Agnes Whistling Elk
Flight of the Seventh Moon

July 2

True Marriage

It is hard, very hard indeed, to maintain balance in a patriarchal world as a woman. If you can truly marry, then you can be a living example to your sisters and the society you live in. I mean not just a marriage

U

fixated on the body, but a true marriage of the soul, where true intimacy is born. Balance begins in your own circle. Your life is then an art, and that is the best position from which to teach.

Agnes Whistling Elk
Star Woman

July 3

Negativity

A little while ago you thought you had driven into hell. I was negative and pessimistic and dark. All I could see were the bad aspects of my life. I separated myself by my attitude and created a very lonely broken country, a hard place to be. Ruby and I did this in order to show you that your world is exactly as you create it. You can choose to see nothing but darkness and pain. Surely it is there and needs to be acknowledged. But not in a negative way. If there is no gas, you go earn money to get gas. Or you change the pathway and find heat from another source. I don't know if you noticed, but the wind shook and went crazy when all that was happening. I was locked in an outpouring of negativity that poisoned the atmosphere around me. No matter what you said or did, it would have been wrong, because I was behind the shadow barrier that neither you nor I could climb. Many people are trapped in that place of pain. Beware. It marks your burial, the death of your dreams, and the beginning of sorrows.

Agnes Whistling Elk
Star Woman

July 4

You Can Give Away Your Power— That's Your Choice

A magical child of light is preparing to be born. All forms of life, even if they are imbalanced and dark, fight to survive. That is why we feel resistance. The womb is giving birth to the time of the child. It means that we are all responsible for the reality that surrounds us. We make our own problems; they don't happen to us. If you are giving away your power or not, you are still responsible. What anyone does on this earth is remembered. Now you will reap the effects of your acts. That is the meaning of the child.

Ani
Windhorse Woman

July 5

Follow Your Heart

I am she who nourishes. I am she who walks with you to show you the road. Through me, you can be initiated. Through me, you can taste victory. Walk last and pick up the burdens of the people. No woman is worthy until she follows her heart.

Yellow Robe, as recounted by Agnes
Flight of the Seventh Moon

You Have No Barriers

No barrier will stop a stealthy being. Where the footsteps of the stealthy being disappear, you see a crow or a balloon or an eagle, but what you are really seeing is a stealthy being levitating. The problem with the incapable beings is that they never look at the multiple parts of the tangled trails. They have no knowledge, and that is good—they wouldn't know what to do with it if they had it.

Agnes Whistling Elk
Medicine Woman

July 7

Mate With Your Spirit Warrior

We are all looking for that warrior or warrioress that dwells within us. A man looks for his warrioress, and a woman looks for her warrior. And when she finds him, she mates with him. She mates with him in the physical and she mates with him in spirit. When she can accomplish that, she becomes whole.

Agnes Whistling Elk
The Woman of Wyrrd

July 8

Power Is in Movement

Even though our heava, our dark side, is our wildness unexpressed, it is also the cause of our inability to let go of our egos. You have to learn to walk out of your self lodge and never look back. The self lodge of the ego is not where you live. Your movement on the path between the self lodge and your dream lodge is the way to your understanding of who you are. Power is in the action, the transit, the movement between the many lodges of your own private village.

Agnes Whistling Elk
Star Woman

July 9

Hold a Stone—Who Does It Remind You Of?

The eyes of a rock are a thousand times better than yours or mine. Rocks had to develop that power. You can learn from most stones. Many rocks come from other worlds. Like meteors do. With them you can see the children of the stars. Many of those meteorites are lost and want to go home. If you comfort them, they will show you brilliant worlds where few dare go. If you had eyes like the stones, you could explore the universe and both the future and the past.

Agnes Whistling Elk
Flight of the Seventh Moon

July 10

Never Compete

When the shield carrier reaches the top of the mountain, she never seeks approval, because approval is based on doubt. A shield carrier has no expectations, is never awed by anything, has no beliefs,

U

makes no judgments or comparisons. A shield carrier never competes. She considers herself in opposition with an opponent, not competition.

Agnes Whistling Elk
Flight of the Seventh Moon

July 11

Turning the Can

"We see things because of light. If there was no light then we would see nothing. Perhaps then nothing would exist. Perhaps then all there is is light. Let's make an agreement. That you are this tin can. Then you are reflecting light from one side and not from the other. You see, you are half light. Darkness defines the borders of your light. It is that darkness that you are still unfamiliar with."

Agnes started turning the can so that the shaded part was now illuminated.

"See, the dark side is now light and the light side is now dark. That's all. Everything is a circle. One side

U

supports the other side, so that a whole can will be born. It's very simple and nothing to be afraid of. Your light is your wisdom and understanding. The darkness on this can is formed by the absence of light. To understand your dark side is really only a process of turning the can."

Agnes Whistling Elk
Crystal Woman

July 12

Simplicity

The old ones I used to know said keep it simple. I have seen you stumble over simplicity. You have learned great pyramids of knowledge. But if that learning is not exercised through experience, it cannot be realized. You are like someone with a new pickup truck and a new set of tools. Your truth is your tools. When you set out for the day's work, you leave your tools in the back of your pickup. Simple. You don't use them in the total circle of your life. Like most people, you don't experience with your whole self. That is the difference between knowledge and wisdom.

Agnes Whistling Elk
Flight of the Seventh Moon

July 13

Reflect in Quietness

Time, eons of time, passed in every moment. I was struggling to see more clearly. I lay down flat on the warm rock and extended my consciousness into the water as if I were slowly turning beneath the tides. Like a fish beneath the surface of the ocean, I was lulled into slumber. I rolled back and forth under the sun, quietly resting on the crest of the sea, unable to change my course or instincts.

I wandered effortlessly through submerged caverns, nudging the lifeless forms silhouetted against the ancient rocks as if begging for a sign. I examined my reflection in underground pools for the clue to being alive that was always lost when I came back to shore. I was a creature beyond love or hope. I went back into the caverns beneath the surface alone, crying out to the resemblance of a distant god. I recalled my ancient souls and the turnings and torture that had brought me here. I questioned the very soul of the sea within me. It was the beginning, the wisdom of all ages, serenity and truth there in the tide. The water slipped through my fingers, ripples were born and died, bubbles and foam floated away. In the green water, there was quietness. The surface became sky and cloud, and I was left alone at the edge of the shore.

Lynn
Medicine Woman

July 14

Erasing Anxiety

One day there will come a time when all your anxiety is gone. That is when your goddesshood will become most radiant. That is when you will become like the stars. We have talked about returning to the stars. But you can never return to the stars until all

U

anxiety is gone. If you begin to witness your anxieties instead of reacting to them, you will begin to realize that perhaps there is a pot of gold at the end of the rainbow. Perhaps, in fact, there is relief and there is true beauty in this human life of ours.

Grandmother
The Woman of Wyrrd

July 15

Life Is No Accident

Every act has meaning. Can't you see that? That's what tracking is all about. Accident is a word born of confusion. It means we didn't understand ourselves enough to know why we did something. Accident is a way to lay down the responsibility for your action and ask another to pick it up.

Agnes Whistling Elk
Medicine Woman

July 16

True Power Is Love

Let me explain what I mean by power. That is a word whose meaning has been twisted in your world. When you say power, people become afraid. They think of the police and the tax collectors and someone having power over them. That is not what I mean by power. Power, in my way, is the understanding of the spirit of energy that flows through all beings. A shaman person can translate that energy into healing and transformation for herself or others. Power is strength and the ability to see yourself through your own eyes and not through the eyes of another. It is being able to place a circle of power at your own feet and not take power from someone else's circle. True power is love.

Agnes Whistling Elk
Flight of the Seventh Moon

July 17

Shape Shifter

Twin Dreamers smashed the clock. She is a woman who has smashed time. By dissolving her ego, she can take on the shape of other egos. She has perfected this art to such a degree, she can shift her physical shape and become part of another dreamer's dream. How do you know that you're not a shape shifter in one form or another? Maybe you simply don't remember what you are dreaming!

Agnes Whistling Elk
Star Woman

July 18

Weightlessness

It's all a question of weightlessness. There is light and there is light. One kind of light illuminates the shadows, and another kind of light illuminates the spirit. Weightlessness has to do with your mind. Your body is your mind. It is matter. It has weight and substance. When you move into higher consciousness,

U

when your soul becomes illuminated for all time, you will be in a state of weightlessness. When you move into emptiness, you move into that process. You begin to let go of the body. You let go of the mind and its control over your thoughts, your emotions, and your physical self. When a leaf leaves its mother tree, when it floats off the branch and into the air—it is as if its spirit takes flight. In a sense it has let go of its connections with its body, with its larger physical self, and has moved into the source of power. Weightlessness is learning to be without form.

Shakkai
Shakkai, Woman of the Sacred Garden

July 19

Mind

Agnes pushed her finger in the middle of the dust spiral. "When you are born, you come from the void. You come from the mystery. You are born out of formlessness from the center of the spiral. You dress yourself with the fine feathers of time and space, and you take on a mind. You think you are

U

mind. Your earthwalk is a spiraling outward from this center. As you progress, you become more and more earthbound. You take on form through experience and conditioning from your environment. You become encrusted with addictions and what you call time. To stay in form, you must develop a mind that is your ego, which again is a function of time.

Agnes Whistling Elk
Star Woman

July 20

All Life Has a Mouth

There are many mouths of which we are unaware. Everything alive has a big mouth, or else it would be unable to exist. One very important mouth is the one that lives between the two rounds of intention that you call your conscious mind and your unconscious mind. This mouth, like any other mouth, needs food. In the world of shamanism, finding the proper food is everything. Finding the proper food for a spirit will keep it alive. If it's a bad spirit, you'll want to find and take away its proper food, so it will soon move on.

Zoila
Jaguar Woman

July 21

The Food of Greatness Is Humbleness

When you journey out of the ego lodge, you drop away from your worn, everyday path into a helpless state; you become humble. You look around with frightened eyes, and you pray to the Great Spirit. That is a beginning. In your prayer you will find beauty.

Ruby Plenty Chiefs
The Woman of Wyrrd

Never Stand Outside Your Power

You stand here in the center of your being. This point marks the essence of who you are. When you become powerful in life, you stand at the center of your own will and your own intent. There is no one who can move you. You become the immovable one. You become the one who is never outside her power no matter what happens on a physical or a spiritual plane.

Grandmother
The Woman of Wyrrd

July 23

La Caldera

Because of my fear of heights, my mind didn't want my body to continue. But some deep longing made me willing to follow Zoila. It was as if all my concepts of self had exploded in my head, leaving me with only my willpower to help me survive. My mind and its fear were useless on this precarious

U

pathway. I was battling with my conception of who I was and what I could do. Knowing I couldn't do it, I did it anyway. This process produced a numbness of thought, so my fear did not paralyze me. As we slowly traversed around and down, I became more sure of myself, letting go of my first level of terror. As we went farther, other, deeper levels of terror became released, until an ecstatic feeling flooded through my being.

Lynn in La Caldera
Jaguar Woman

July 24

Be a Guiding Light for Others

There are times when you have to think just about yourself. There are times when it is not a bad thing to be selfish; there are times when it helps you be strong. If you are not strong, if you cannot make your way in the world, then you cannot be an example for other women.

Grandmother
The Woman of Wyrrd

July 25

Sit in the Eye of the Storm

Look at the pond. The water is clear and perceptive. You are becoming like the water. There is a new stillness. See that breeze there rippling on the surface of the pond. The chaos of life moves over you like a wind. You are becoming like a quiet pond. You reflect the chaos on the surface, but within you are still.

Ruby Plenty Chiefs
Windhorse Woman

July 26

Plants Give Signs

All plants have talents. Some can be used to heal bruises, some can lower a temperature, some can intoxicate you, and so forth. That is their ability and their purpose on earth. We are different from plants. A plant knows what its life is about from the moment it sprouts as a seedling. We humans, on the other hand, are only a possibility when we are born. We must discover our purpose and meaning and then we must find the courage to follow that purpose. Some plants have the ability to give signs; they can mark our path. As a woman of power, you need only learn how to follow the trail.

Agnes Whistling Elk
Crystal Woman

July 27

Be Connected, Not Addicted

You are now walking into the sacred mountains where the bear dances with the white-plumed arrows. You have heard the dreamers. Emotions are born the moment you are connected to something, and you are connected to the dreamers. Follow the right trail and become one thing. Become a woman. In your world, womanhood is lost.

Agnes Whistling Elk
Medicine Woman

Listen to the Earth Breathing

Listen and feel the earth breathing beneath you. Listen carefully to her, lay down on her, and one day you will become an earth prophetess. You will be able to see the weather before it comes, six months away. You will sense rain and thunder and disasters before they occur. She will talk to you. To learn this better, open the energy centers within your own body. See the red of the center at the base of your spine. Then move up to the orange in your lower belly, then to yellow in your solar plexus, and on up your body to the top of your head.

Agnes Whistling Elk
Flight of the Seventh Moon

July 29

Remember Who You Are

The film in a camera is forever obsessed with the thought of you. Your face is imprinted on its memory forever. The film clings to your image. It is ob-

U

sessed with you. A mirror reflects your image, but it is different from the film that also reflects your face. The mirror is not obsessed with the past like the film. The mirror reflects life, whatever is placed in front of it. When that reality shifts and changes, the mirror is left unchanged. Mirrors can change us greatly, because they enable us to see things that we may not have noticed. Like spinach caught between our teeth or the dark side of the soul. But the mirror never changes. The mirror is the sacred witness to everything that chooses to be reflected within its sphere. It has much to teach you.

Ani
Windhorse Woman

July 30

Spirit into Substance

What you put in your bundle is self-understanding from your own personal visions, and it is a part of your truth, no other. In making a personal bundle you take something intangible—a feeling, a dream,

U

even a problem—from inside yourself, and you manifest it into the physical world so that you can examine it and use it. This process of transformation from spirit into substance enables you to heal others, because through your action of making it, you heal yourself.

Agnes Whistling Elk
Jaguar Woman

July 31

The Only Thing to Fear Is Fear Itself

I remembered Agnes's words in Nepal when I had been so frightened by a healer in the foothills of the Himalayas. "Sorcerers never kill you," she had said. "They make you kill yourself." And I thought: Yes, you give away your power because of your own terror and your own fear.

Lynn
Shakkai, Woman of the Sacred Garden

August 1

Silence

The only true communion is without words. Language is a barrier between us, but we need to talk for many reasons, not necessarily to understand much. Silence is the only true source of communication, like you and the stone. You communed with each other from the essence of yourself. Form was the only difference between you. I know you and Agnes have moved into the mysteries of silence many times. I want you to see the agreements we make, the links in the chain that represent the way we think we give and take knowledge; how we move from one end of that chain to the other. Do you have more knowledge at the end of a lifetime of linking one thought to another, or do you just end up at the end of the chain, like you started?

Ani
Windhorse Woman

August 2

The Final Mother

When women understand their Ultima Madre, or final mother, they can build altars and fetishes of these powers. When they feel the influence of Crazy Woman or the Death Mother, in the form of depression or gloom, they can light candles and burn copal and honor her great power, the dark side. You see, her intent only defines your goodness and beauty. By honoring the dark side, you destroy her power over you. Then she can't take you.

Zoila
Jaguar Woman

August 3

Are You a Queen or a Princess?

There is one egg that you would do well to hatch— one that is in harmony with the Great Spirit. It is the sacred rock at the center of the hoop. Hatch the sacred rock and you will hatch the queen bird that rips her talons through all the barriers to perception.

U

Whether you believe me or not, hatch the idea that the hoop of the self is also the hoop of the universe. For you are the queen bird that soars on forever, limitless, and have no boundaries. Only the queen bird builds a true nest, without separations.

Agnes Whistling Elk
Medicine Woman

August 4

Truth Is Always the Same

The truth is always the same. Truth is what is. No matter what name you give it, what religion you call it, the truth is that the great beings, the conscious beings that have been on this planet are reflections of the Old One, reflections of God. The religions that are built around them often do not accurately pass on what the great teachers taught. It is important for you to see that truth is the same throughout the ages. It makes no difference what time or place you live in. What matters is that you become enlightened, and that is truly all that matters.

Grandmother
The Woman of Wyrrd

U

Experience New Ways

In our world, we form a hand—five shaman women or five shaman men. With the hand you have the numbers, life, unity, equality, eternity, teacher. They add up to perfection. In women's councils we change positions so each person experiences these other positions and can become a total person—there is growth in change.

Ruby Plenty Chiefs
Flight of the Seventh Moon

If Today Were Your Last Day, What Would You Do?

If you are afraid of death, you will not live your life. You will be immersed in your addictions to fears, to phantoms in the night.

Ani
Windhorse Woman

August 7

Celebrate Your Moon Time

For so long the memory of her who gives us life has been hidden. We forget that our moon is our celebration time for her life within us. Women in their moon have set themselves aside because it is their power time, their time to look within and feed their inner strength. In the old way there were special lodges for women in their moon, and most women of the camp would bleed near the same time. That is because our bodies adapt to the harmony of our sisters. In those days we slept and rose with the sun. Our working hours were the same, and you could say that we bled together because of the light of Grandmother Sun—in those days she was Grandmother, not Grandfather.

Agnes Whistling Elk
Flight of the Seventh Moon

August 8

Balance of the Male and Female

Men and women need each other; we need to learn from each other. That's part of what this life is all about.

Zoila
Jaguar Woman

August 9

Mind as Ruler

You're stuck because you think too much. You think your knowledge is going to get you out of the mess you're in. You believe you're going to master the situation with your mind. You don't listen to your will, and you are full of fear. Listen to your entirety, your total self. We have trouble finding our way back to the center of the spiral because we have enthroned the mind. As long as the mind is the ruler, you will spend your life stuck in a swamp.

Zoila
Jaguar Woman

U

Vulnerability Is a Great Defense

The flow of the water empties me of myself. I sit here in spirit waiting for the world and my people to stop fighting. In anger and war there is only hardness. People and the world become solid, and they forget the river. They forget how to flow. To find the river of your spirit is to find freedom. There is no need to come up against anyone. When you become rigid in the world, then the world has no more need of you, and your spirit slowly drains away like blood spilled onto sand. Just float with the water, and let the Great Spirit flow with you.

Agnes Whistling Elk
The Woman of Wyrrd

August 11

Power Wheels

Listen to me—I'll tell you a story from the ancient sacred belts. A long time ago, the power wheels were in outer space. They were beautiful and had every

U

power except one. They could not touch. The power wheels looked down and they saw Mother Earth. They saw many creatures who could touch but had no feeling. The power wheels said to one another, "Why don't we go down and enter into those creatures' bodies so that their egos can feel and so the power wheels can touch. Look, down there are all those creatures walking around who cannot know each other." So the power wheels went down and filled those creatures' bodies.

Agnes Whistling Elk
Flight of the Seventh Moon

August 12

Define Your Prey

Before you can be an effective warrioress, you must become an expert huntress—the great warrioress was beforehand a great huntress. Being a huntress is very complicated. There are many creatures to hunt. You can hunt and trap a spirit if you know how. There are spirit traps you can make. Spirits are hidden from

U

you—you think they are born in your imagination. But the imagination can turn on you and kill you if you don't know how to look at it straight.

Agnes Whistling Elk
Medicine Woman

August 13

Mud

"See, my daughter, as you well know, this lotus blossom for a long time germinated in the mud, out of the mud into the light of day, into the magnificent, innocent flower that you see before you."

"I don't understand," I said.

"The chaos of life, the madness, the pain, the agony, the evil that surrounds the human condition on so many levels, is represented by the mud."

Shakkai and O Kiku
Shakkai, Woman of the Sacred Garden

U

Woman Is the Keeper of the Earth

The Star Nations brought this extraordinary knowledge onto our planet. It was lost to most people, but it was memorized all over the world by women. Women are the keepers of the ancient knowledge, and we are the keepers of Mother Earth, because we share her energy, because we share her source of power. Because of our connection with Mother Earth, it is fitting for women to preserve this knowledge.

Agnes Whistling Elk
The Woman of Wyrrd

August 15

Movement

We are built of fibers and between each and every being that is alive is a network of fibers not unlike this spider web. It is important to understand this, because if I move here, if I do a movement here in my mind, in my emotions, with my energy physically, or simply with my spirit shield, in one way or another it affects someone living on the other side of the country. Any movement I make produces corresponding movement over there. I am affected in the same way, when that person moves or sends out a positive or negative thought.

Grandmother
The Woman of Wyrrd

August 16

Carry Your Self Shield Proudly

There are shields for practically everything. Shields are not only for defense. They stand as a record of who you are in the world in all your aspects—mental, emotional, physical, and spiritual. They stand for your sacredness within. They can be placed outside the lodges to tell people who you are.

Agnes Whistling Elk
Flight of the Seventh Moon

U

Honor Your Child Self

This shield is called Destroyer-of-Children. It is a good shield, a shield with much dignity and meaning. Whenever a man kills the child within himself and hates his deadness and begins to treat innocent children harmfully, it is a very bad thing. The first law, my daughter, is that all power comes from woman. The second law is never to do anything that harms children. Always protect the children.

Agnes Whistling Elk
Flight of the Seventh Moon

August 18

Follow Your Dreams

A dreamer is one who knows how to enter the sacred round and exit at will. The sacred rounds, and there are seven, are controlled by the katchina powers. The first round is normal everyday life, the world you live in and the way you normally perceive it. The second round is sleep. The third round is where the dreamers

U

go. It is called walking through the gateway between the worlds. Understand this, you only go between the worlds. If you were in them, you would be spirit, and that would be what we call death.

Agnes Whistling Elk
Medicine Woman

August 19

Understand with Your Heart

What we do not understand we want to destroy. That is the human tragedy.

Grandmother
The Woman of Wyrrd

August 20

Conquering Maya

Every once in a while a great teacher comes. Great teachers are the realized ones. They are the noble chiefs and leaders who have conquered all illusion, all maya. They have climbed the Tree and have achieved

U

freedom. They have solved the riddle of paradox and duality. They can speak only truth. But even they have difficulty in trying to explain things in a way others can understand. Some of them get mad and use supernatural powers all over the place, thinking that this may help. Others martyr themselves to show their great love and tolerance. Some of them don't do anything at all and let everything go on as it is. They may be hidden in a cave or sacred mountain, or they may be your next-door neighbor.

Agnes Whistling Elk
Jaguar Woman

August 21

Darkness Defines the Light

Don't you understand that darkness defines the light? None of us is perfect. We are striving for perfection. By denying the darkness of our own souls, we create a negative energy in the world. All of us have felt jealousy and greed. All of us have lost our way at one time or another. It is a very good thing to witness someone else walking down the wrong path. If there is love in your heart, you will do what you can to bring that person back to harmony and balance in life.

Shakkai
Shakkai, Woman of the Sacred Garden

August 22

Butterfly Tree

The ancients have wisely spoken of the sacred tree. Almost all peoples know of some kind of world tree. The tree is a way into life. It's a person's destiny to realize that we are one with the sacred tree. We are not just a leaf. We are light. And we are the light of Butterfly Tree. Everything is of Butterfly Tree, and all will return to it. All suffering is a result of a loss of knowledge of our origins. When we realize that we are the great tree, our state is happiness. All your illusions come about because of loss of remembering the central tree.

Agnes Whistling Elk
Jaguar Woman

August 23

We Cannot Lose One Another

There are many things that you still do not know, but as you are able to travel the dimensions of the universe, as you are able to avail yourself of the energy of the stars and Mother Earth and the harmony of all that lives, you will begin to see that all of life is a circle, that all beings that are alive are part of that circle, that in fact, though we become lost in the dream of duality, the dream of separateness, we are in fact all reflections of the Great Spirit. We are all indeed part of the same spirit and the same God. We are indeed all one. We cannot lose each other on any level, but sometimes in our ignorance we forget the meaning of life, and we forget our destiny. What we do together is a process of remembering, of remembering who we truly are.

Agnes Whistling Elk
The Woman of Wyrrd

U

August 24

Waken

Waken within yourself. You are the black wolf instead of the white wolf, because you wear the black cloak of contemplation. If you were the white wolf, you would be more outward, more extroverted. You track through the forests for what you want and then come back to the pack and curl up in the sun and think about it. You're a lone wolf who is afraid of being alone.

Agnes Whistling Elk to Lynn
Medicine Woman

August 25

Power Dances

When power comes to you, be still with her. Don't discuss it and bleed the energy away. Just hold it. Slowly she will begin to dance with you, but only if you are patient and listen for her voice.

Zoila
Jaguar Woman

August 26

Mirror the Goddess

It is important for you to know who you are. Trust me. I will tell you of your limitations. But it is important that you remember who you are. Women today—wherever they are in the world, through all our centuries of learning, through all of this time of revolution—still do not remember our goddess selves deep within. I am here to mirror that extraordinary image that you are.

Shakkai
Shakkai, Woman of the Sacred Garden

August 27

Dream Your Vision

You must understand that the dreamers have chosen you. Remember the wolf fur that I gave you when I drew you the map? Don't ever sleep without it, because powers other than the dreamers will try to harm you. The wolf fur will protect you. As the huntress you are also the hunted. You must understand that will is not a mystery. It is simple. Will dreams the balance and empowers the mind. What are your night visions or your pain but the failure of your will? I have to go now. I leave you within the mirror of creativity and touching the world circle.

Grey Wolf
Medicine Woman

August 28

Reflect Each Other

We're like the water. If we're the lake—as I see you in me—I'm in you. We're the great mirror. We're nothing but the reflection of each other. If I didn't have anybody around, I would only have myself to define myself.

Ruby Plenty Chiefs
Flight of the Seventh Moon

August 29

Find the Aspects of Self That You Have Given Away

Never forget that this life, this dream that we are, is a chimera, a reflection of what can be real and total. Keep on struggling with your lost reflections.

Agnes Whistling Elk
Windhorse Woman

August 30

Negativity

When you have a negative thought, it steals your life force to some degree. Haven't you ever wondered why you get tired and depressed when you think about certain things? It's because you've created a parasite, like mistletoe, which lives off another life source—you. Because of that, it has the potential to kill you.

Agnes Whistling Elk
Jaguar Woman

August 31

Follow Your Destiny

I'm a medicine woman. I live in the beyond and come back, and you went there with me last night. You are being initiated into a knowledge as old as time. The dreamers have touched you. Sometimes you can look back over your shoulder and not pay any attention. You can choose to be blind, or you can follow your destiny.

Agnes Whistling Elk
Medicine Woman

September 1

Caring

There are many kinds of caring. Just like alcohol or drugs or addictive relationships, you can be addicted to caring to the point that it pulls you off center. Caring is important, but it is only part of the whole of who you are. You cannot care so much that it becomes an obsession. You must see the totality of things and realize where your caring, like everything else, fits into the perspective of your life. Emotions are important; all of what you feel and think is important, because these things make you who you are. Negative ideas are parts of you that need to be honored, so that they can then be healed and brought back into balance.

Agnes Whistling Elk
Shakkai, Woman of the Sacred Garden

U

September 2

Do Not Misuse Your Power

A black sorcerer is always seduced by his own vision of greed and fear. The only way to make a sorcerer change his ways is for him to begin to see that power will eventually turn on those who misuse it.

Jaguar Woman
Jaguar Woman

September 3

See the Light Around You

True knowledge has always been hidden, given only to those who are worthy of it. It has to be that way. There are many secrets and many of them are coming to light in your time.

Agnes Whistling Elk
Medicine Woman

September 4

Beyond Imagination

What happened to you today happened to all of you. That's why it was magical, and that is why you became intoxicated. You dreamed beyond imagination into the space reserved for shamans, for seers. That lonely world where madness and genius meet is familiar to a person of power. You are destined to walk there in the great mysteries of this dimension. Never think that you found this path simply because you have worked hard and long and through many lifetimes. You are now and forever on the ultimate journey, the greatest adventure—following your way down the path of heart.

Agnes Whistling Elk
Flight of the Seventh Moon

September 5

Use Your Vision

Understand that it is what you choose not to observe in your life that controls your life.

Butterfly Woman
Jaguar Woman

September 6

Take Courage

I once asked Agnes what she thought about the biblical expression, "Many are called but few are chosen." She laughed and said that we are all called and we are all chosen if we simply have the courage to step into the unknown.

Lynn
Flight of the Seventh Moon

September 7

Woman Carries the Void

Woman is the ultimate. Mother Earth belongs to woman, not man. She carries the void.

Agnes Whistling Elk
Medicine Woman

September 8

There Are Two Ways of Looking

There are some things you can't explain with words. That's why you must learn two ways of looking— one with your eyes and one with your dream body.

Agnes Whistling Elk
Flight of the Seventh Moon

U

September 9

What Mask Are You Wearing?

You can change your face by leaving yourself open or by putting on a mask. Mask-making is an ancient shaman art. There are many kinds of masks. There are masks of people—warriors, dead shamans, masks that embody the spirit of animals and hunting objects; there are guardian spirit masks; and there are masks that stand up with the spirit of the sun or moon or the heart of a great hunter like the wolf. These masks can be magical and can bring powers in any endeavor, be it hunting, dancing for rain, fertile crops, or gifts within the mysteries of healing and dreaming.

Agnes Whistling Elk
Flight of the Seventh Moon

September 10

Be Aware

Everything you need is here. The things you need are always here; you need to be smart enough to find them.

Agnes Whistling Elk
Jaguar Woman

September 11

Dreams

Dreams and visions are the essence of sacredness.

Zoila
Jaguar Woman

September 12

Power Bundle

Remember the importance of saying what you need to say. If you hold your power in your throat, I will have to return and I can cause your throat to hurt very much. Make a throat bundle for your altar. Take the visions that you have had. Make an image of these feelings and things you have experienced. Pray with it. Put power into it. Do a ceremony, and you will have a bundle that has power. It is a gift, a blessing from the Great Spirit. He sends this knowledge so that you may live.

Little Green Man to Lynn
Jaguar Woman

September 13

Springs of Magic

The springs of magic and wet places of power are running dry. Come drink of this clean water from this spring.

Butterfly Woman
Jaguar Woman

September 14

Honor Power When You Meet Power

Each person has her own power. Honor each person and salute the power shield within her.

Ruby Plenty Chiefs
Flight of the Seventh Moon

September 15

Growth

You have already died to who you were. Everything is the same and nothing is the same. Now you truly see.

Butterfly Woman
Jaguar Woman

U

September 16

Look into the Mirrors You Have Created in Life

Truth is the only purity. The energy that you have been feeling is a kind of truth; in actuality it is a force. Most people on earth think that the physical world and the spirit world are combined, that they are one and the same. They also think that force or energy is part of the material world and is usually produced by it. Look at a crystal; it is a perfect example. It represents a crystallized form of spirit, because it is of the material realm. Force, on the other hand, is spirit that has not yet been crystallized into a physical form. The rainbows emanating from the crystal are the color of force that is more dense than spirit and not yet a form. The music of the earth mother sings to us through color. When you see form, you see color. And when you see color, you see music and tones in their solid form. The force that has been felt in your dreams is a pervading energy that people the world over are feeling and do not understand. They experience this energy as a quickening. Their

U

lives are moving faster and they can barely keep up with their shifts in consciousness and the needs of everyday life. They don't understand that spirit is increasing their needs so that new mirrors can be formed. These mirrors are teachers if only the people will have the courage to look into them and learn.

Ani
Windhorse Woman

September 17

Remember Your Dreams

Don't you think the moon lodge is real? Dreams are diving down deep in the earth. They are feminine in character. Male takes the substance and forms it. Dreams are your other-half vision. Don't you think you are real? This time you brought back power. This time you remembered.

Agnes Whistling Elk
Medicine Woman

September 18

What You Choose Not to Look at Rules Your Life

The trees and animals are no less alive than we are. I have been taught that all of life is part of God, or Danu. Danu is love and light, and we are reflections of that great light. Danu is sometimes darkness, and sometimes we also reflect that aspect of her.

Grandmother
The Woman of Wyrrd

September 19

Live Your Truth

You are full of words and borrowed knowledge from your social system. That has its purpose. But here we make you live what we want you to learn. That's why we change personalities. Because we are the teaching. We don't stand up at a podium and lecture you about truth. We make you feel and breathe truth, become it. You have to react to our play and that starts you down a road.

Agnes Whistling Elk
Flight of the Seventh Moon

September 20

Bone-Keeper Doll

The bone-keeper doll represents your life. The spirit lives in your bones. It holds your good intentions, the things that you want to accomplish in this lifetime. Your spiritual and earth-plane goals are part of the body of the bone-keeper doll. Remember that the bone-keeper represents your hopes and future accomplishments.

Agnes Whistling Elk
Star Woman

U

September 21

The Way of the Warrioress

The butterfly is beautiful only for its season. Like a warrioress, she touches the world briefly with her iridescent wings and then becomes transformed into another form of life, as will you.

Butterfly Woman
Jaguar Woman

FALL

September 22

Touch the Earth

Has it ever occurred to you that the human is teetering between two worlds of reflection? Touch the earth, for the mother is awake. The earth is alive and dreaming. Everything the human can think of has substance. There are no holes in your thoughts. The awake ones, the shamaness can wander to the other side of the universe, beyond even the far-away. Here appears the rainbow door to the backward web of substance. If you invade that world, the beings there can give you any power you want. Most powers are too heavy to bring back. How glad we are if we can get back through that door once it's been opened to us. But the greatest warriors have counted coup there many times. You came here through that door the moment you were conceived and you are sucked back through it the moment you die. That is where it is all given and that is where it is all taken away. The keepers want you to come there and take what you can. When you enter, they recognize you and sing and chant. You speak of substance. Listen, every substance, including my dreams, is my sister and my brother, and I recognize them and we live here gently.

Agnes Whistling Elk
Medicine Woman

September 23

Becoming

If you are always becoming your whole life through, and suddenly there is nothing left to become, you are filled with terror. Because becoming is your life distraction, and suddenly you are face-to-face with your own empty being. It's like sitting down to a great feast and realizing it is a banquet for the dead. And you are the only one eating. You want to run from the feast, but where are you to go?

Agnes Whistling Elk
Star Woman

September 24

Be a Worthy Opponent

"It's a very great thing to have an opponent."

"What do you mean?"

"Say you were a writer and you decided to pick Anaïs Nin as your worthy opponent. You tried to beat her in creativity and ideas. In a sense, you would use her to see yourself. You don't want her to fail— you would lose your model. What does a person of power want you to do? They want to give away to you until you have power so that you can become a worthy opponent to another worthy warrior."

Agnes Whistling Elk and Lynn
Medicine Woman

September 25

Everything Is Possible

I have taught you something new, and that is the trail out of depression. When you work with people who are troubled, teach them something new. Not only does it bring them out of a destructive mood, but it centers them. It changes them, like poetry, like a beautiful work of art. When a shaman works with you, he or she works on the tapestry of your life, helping you tie new knots, bring in new colors to your design, and when that happens, your heart opens and all of life becomes possible again.

Agnes Whistling Elk
Shakkai, Woman of the Sacred Garden

September 26

Life Force Is Like Music

Music is like life. The song that you heard was here for just a moment, and now it is gone somewhere else. It has moved away for someone else to enjoy. Our life force moves through us like this melody.

Shakkai
Shakkai, Woman of the Sacred Garden

Lie Back into the Arms
of the Great Mother

I am a mirror for you, as is Ruby, and as is Grandmother. We are mirrors for different parts of you that
need to grow. Those mirrors will be there for you as
long as you need them, and then when you need
them one day no longer, we merge together like
pieces of a puzzle finding their place interlocked with
one another. It is all truth, and it is all light. We are
that. Lie back into the arms of the Great Mother, and
let her guide your path.

Agnes Whistling Elk
The Woman of Wyrrd

September 28

Where Is Home?

You learn as much as you're capable of learning. You have all that you need in this lifetime to become enlightened; whether that happens or not is really up to you.

Agnes Whistling Elk
The Woman of Wyrrd

September 29

Live with Danger

This woman of power is going against the grain of the wood. She is swimming upstream against the current. That creates a very unusual and powerful energy of its own kind. A female warrior knows how to use that energy. By being a woman in this male-oriented life, she is changing the direction of the current, just by being a woman in this position. When enough women swim against the current, it will change the current forever. Then if she becomes a warrior, she has double the power and twice the energy. Once she knows how to use it to her advantage, she knows how to live with danger. She is dangerous herself. She is living with vision among people who have eyes but cannot see. They will want to blind her and take away her vision. She is preserving a tradition that is ancient, sacred, and unknown to most. The female warrior knows that life is an adventure of the spirit. She knows that this earthwalk is only a dream born of a greater dream beyond our imagination.

Twin Dreamers
Star Woman

September 30

We Are in a War Against Ignorance

The Book of the Child contains a history of higher thought and a history of thought to come. The history is a remembrance of patterns. Truth is in the patterns and meanings, not the words or events that make up that meaning. The patterns are there and can be read. The child has been conceived and will be born. The star seeds have been planted and we are all responsible for their care. No longer can we hide behind the veils of ignorance. With the birth of the child, the veils of ignorance will be torn away.

Ani
Windhorse Woman

October 1

Conception

When the sacred wheels come down it is called conception. At conception the light becomes brilliant and then chooses a color. I always know when a woman has conceived—because of the large and small lights. Power has entered her body. At death the wheel returns to outer space and the earthbound body returns to Mother Earth.

Agnes Whistling Elk
Flight of the Seventh Moon

October 2

Mind Is Ego

Time is born of what you call the ego and what we call the self lodge. The ego is the illusion of form. To remain in form one must have a concept of time because of the similarity of the two. Time is a construct of the mind, because the mind is ego. It desperately holds onto time and clutches it like a tyrant, because it wants to survive. Once you leap the boundaries of time and step into timelessness, you step into the sacred dream wheel, where the ego is no longer needed. The ego is an entity that struggles for survival and fears the loss of form, because it knows it will die.

Agnes Whistling Elk
Jaguar Woman

October 3

You Are the Center

"I feel almost pregnant. Those babies—are they still inside me?"

"They have always been within you and within all women. Remember, everything must be born of woman. It is a power the world has forgotten. Men are interlopers. Many people, including some of my people, do not understand and would be angry for my words. Nevertheless, it is law. Woman is the flowering tree. You are the center of the universe, of creation, the Mother Earth. You needed to relearn this and build up your strength. Now your training can begin."

Lynn and Agnes Whistling Elk
Medicine Woman

October 4

Burst Through

It is not easy to walk the earth as a power woman, a healer, yea. You are bursting through the last of the old crust on your previous layer of existence. You must fight for what you need to learn. You are in a new land, in the heart of you and with your feet. Listen with great care and watch where you step. Your very life depends on it.

Ginevee
Crystal Woman

October 5

Show Respect

Grandfather Mountain is very old. He was very sacred to the ancestors. He will be here a long time and he has seen many things. Always show respect and honor by giving him tobacco before you come here. He calls out to many kinds of power and many kinds of power answer him. Here, within the ancient wheel, many new powers are born. This circle is the earthly shield of the sky beings. May their four winds blow gently on you for all the years to come. May they illuminate your shields.

Agnes Whistling Elk
Flight of the Seventh Moon

October 6

Chrysalis

They said that the Great Spirit had made the butterfly to show us how to live. The life of the caterpillar transforms into another life—the beautiful butterfly. It teaches us that all of life is transitory. The butterfly is enlightened! Another gift from the Great Spirit. You see, they are the ancestor spirits, and they have returned to the Butterfly Tree. The Great Spirit permits these beings before they leave this world to return one last time to the places of the ceremonies, the sacred places, where as humans they had found great joy. Where the butterflies cluster on a tree, this was one of the ancient sites where rituals and ceremonies were performed, places of celebration.

Agnes Whistling Elk
Jaguar Woman

October 7

Life Is a Schoolhouse

Life is a great game and a dangerous one and a fatal one. It is a game that is painful for all of us. It is not easy to be human, and we have all chosen this game so that we may learn, so that we may grow into varying stages of enlightenment.

Shakkai
Shakkai, Woman of the Sacred Garden

October 8

Experience the Unknowable Every Day

There is a power in the universe that can be used and learned about. There is a whole world that you have seen only a glimpse of. When you see light around living things, when you know what events are about to happen, when you talk to the birds—that is part of the world of Wyrrd. It is the world of Danu that you do not see. It is the unknowable world.

Grandmother
The Woman of Wyrrd

October 9

Sing Your Power Song

I came from the whirling lake
The lake is my gateway
I stand in the lake and know my death
I am spirit woman
I am word woman
I write of my death in sacred time
Sacred time is born of the lake
I am spirit woman

I bring you light from the faraway
A path lit by Grandmother Moon
I am a gatherer of words
My wolf trails shine from the moon
The whirling lake brings forth my words
I stand in the lake and know my death
Shaman words return your spirit
Lost spirit of the great earth round
I return to the women of mystery
The spirit words that have been lost.

Agnes Whistling Elk
Flight of the Seventh Moon

October 10

Look into Your Mirror and Ask, "Who Am I?"

To become enlightened is to become like a mirror. If you have reflected the sun and then the sun sets, you can happily reflect the moon. We leak most of our power by our attachment to the images we reflect. We are like the film in a camera. If we become a famous jhagrini, or healer, in our life, we become a jhagrini, not a woman living her medicine who happens to have developed the gifts of healing. It is the same for everyone—bankers, doctors, housewives. We never see who we are. We are obsessed with our own reflection.

Ani
Windhorse Woman

October 11

We Are All Part of One Another

The Goddess Mother created us as reflections of herself. God to me is the Great Mother. God to me is the Old One. But it does not really matter; God is God. Life force is life force, and it takes many forms. God is the creator, the Great Spirit that permeates all of us. Once you truly understand that, you realize that we are all part of one another, that we are in agreement on this wonderful, green earth, and that we live in a state of duality, a state of separateness that is not real. We are separated by an agreement called space and time. You can move in and out of the dimensions of time.

Grandmother
The Woman of Wyrrd

October 12

Male-Female Shield

Men teach women how to organize their consciousness, especially out in the everyday world. Women teach men about the sacred dream, how to receive and implement the wisdom of their consciousness. Women teach men how to live. Men teach women how to express their dreams, and bring an exchange of energy back from the world, such as money or food or other material goods.

Zoila
Jaguar Woman

October 13

Rainbow Birds

Your symbol today was the swirl. Some call it the whirling logs or the whirling from which all things are born. What you saw was the gateway to your innocence, a spiral, an opening to the knowledge of your womanhood. The rainbow birds told of the colors of the rainbow—one for each of the ever-widening circles of the spiral and the feather for the shield from Spotted Eagle. The stone woman of the falls blessed you and welcomes you to her world of river stones. Put one in your inner shield.

Agnes Whistling Elk
Flight of the Seventh Moon

October 14

Every Day Is a New Birth

Whether you know it or not, I have been telling you about birth. Birth was when the stones walked out of the earth. Other sacred fires were here before us. The stones are the keepers of the hills. The secrets of the ages are written on the stones from the dawn of birth. Stones are universally used for tools, weapons, rituals, fire beds, medicine stones. Mother Earth was once stone. Now we look around for the pieces.

Agnes Whistling Elk
Flight of the Seventh Moon

October 15

A Sense of Death Is a Great Ally

You have chosen power, Lynn. Power has chosen you. Did I ever say that the shaman way was easy? Death is near you. You two are becoming acquainted. Know each other well. Death is all you have. Only when you understand death can you truly begin to live.

Agnes Whistling Elk
Flight of the Seventh Moon

October 16

Celebrate What You Have Become

Some humans could do things better than others, but no one liked to do the same thing over and over. When the spirit of the doing was captured, we left it at that. We told a good story and we left it at that. We chanted a good chant and left it like that. We sang a good song and let it return. There was an exception—when a thing had power, we kept it. We kept the knowledge.

Agnes Whistling Elk
Medicine Woman

October 17

Activity

You see, this river, this creek, speaks to you of movement. It is life force reflected through the water, and as it flows by you, it, too, tells you of truth. You are surrounded by truth. You are surrounded by your teachers, and the teachers are in nature, in the trees, in the grass that moves in the gentle wind. You see, movement is very different from activity. If you are moving around in a fit of anger, scrambling things, throwing things, stomping around, that is activity. Movement is quite a different thing. It is like an action that comes from the heart and soul of your body. It moves out into the world as an expression of power.

Agnes Whistling Elk
Shakkai, Woman of the Sacred Garden

October 18

We Cannot Explain the Unknowable

People of power know each other by the magnificent light, by the luminous egg that surrounds us. We can see each other and identify each other, but we cannot begin to explain how this happens. We cannot even explain how the spirit shield moves beyond your luminous fibers. We can describe the experience and what it looks like, and that is all. This is the frustration of all people of power.

Agnes Whistling Elk
The Woman of Wyrrd

October 19

Be Receptive to Power

You have made a bid for power, even though you do not know that. Your whole life has been a journey toward discovery, a journey toward wisdom. That is what sets you apart from other people. But power must come to you. It is a gift. And for power to come to you, you must make a place within yourself for that power to live. It must have a home within you.

Grandmother
The Woman of Wyrrd

October 20

Learn the Language of the Night

Both night and day are good. Both speak a language. The language of the night is within you. Most two-leggeds have forgotten the language of night, but it would be good if they remembered, for a long night is coming before the break of dawn. That is the way of the apprentice.

Agnes Whistling Elk
Flight of the Seventh Moon

October 21

Listen to Your Voice

Children are told to speak when spoken to. We as women are taught that to speak of our power is to be shunned by most of society. When you listen to the voices of many men and women, you hear a strangled sound. And it's no wonder. Women's voices are often weak or a monotone or barely audible. Voices need to be open and free, so that energy can flow through the throat center. We hold our enlightenment there. If energy is trapped in the throat, it can't move up into the crown of the head. That's why we get sore throats, thyroid problems, or diseases such as throat cancer. Whenever you have an energy knot like that, it will eventually cause disease.

Agnes Whistling Elk
Jaguar Woman

October 22

Be Proud

Addictions prop you up in a false way. We come here to go back to where we came from. But our mind tells us that we need props to survive. We believe the king we have enthroned. You're too hard on yourself. That's a big addiction for many women. King Brain likes to rack you. Be proud of yourself and what you've accomplished.

Zoila
Jaguar Woman

October 23

To Become Humble Is to Become Great

Beauty and humility both throw you back onto yourself. Everything you experience on this earthwalk is part of a great mirror. Every experience makes you see yourself in a different way. Humbleness is just another mirror. Like beauty, it is an experience that puts you in touch with the Great Spirit. When you are humble you are no longer far away.

You become present, and you do your ceremony or you pray to the Great Spirit for help.

Ruby Plenty Chiefs
The Woman of Wyrrd

October 24

Mirror of the Great Spirit

Women and men of power want to understand the magic of the universe. They want to understand and live within the light of God, within the light of creativity. They want to understand the extraordinary mysteries that encompass our lives, so that they can be more perfect human beings. Truly, we are, each and every one of us, a reflection of God, and that is all that we are. We are mirrors of that great brilliance.

Grandmother
The Woman of Wyrrd

October 25

Sacred Spiral

"That is where we come from," Zoila said in my ear. She pointed at the middle of the whirlpool with her stick. "It is to that mystery we are trying to return."

Zoila
Jaguar Woman

October 26

Dream Your Passion

Dream your passion. Fly away. Go through the hoop of your innermost fears and desires. Meet them and conquer them. Come through your own reflection. Act in your dreams as you want to act and find the guarded kivas where you have hidden your heart.

Agnes Whistling Elk
Medicine Woman

October 27

Power and the Wind

The source of power floats on the wind. The source of power is like the wind itself. It can move mountains and change the surface of the oceans, but it is unseen. You cannot prove it, but you can feel it. It is like magic. Believe in the Great Spirit. Believe in the Tao in the same way. Believe in the integrity of your own soul. Believe in the movement of the winds from the north and the south. Those winds can change the surface of the earth, just as spirit can change the surface of your mind.

Shakkai
Shakkai, Woman of the Sacred Garden

October 28

Love Is Your Destiny

Keep courage, my daughter. Nothing can change the outcome of the race. It has been written in your destiny.

An old woman, talking to Yellow Robe
Flight of the Seventh Moon

October 29

What Are You Becoming?

What is this great Mother Earth dreaming as she turns slowly in her slumber? This dark night seems to never end, and when will she awaken one morning and shrug her shoulders of sleep and wonder and become angry because the bones of her body are being torn apart cell by cell. And what of that dark night within each of us that we cannot learn, but to be broken like an arrow as her great back will be broken if we do not awaken with her. What does the great earth body want with us burdening her? When she bleeds and cleanses herself, will she remember who we are or just what we are becoming?

Agnes Whistling Elk
Flight of the Seventh Moon

October 30

See What's Real

Throw away your juggler eyes and see what's real. People can appear important to you because of one thing or another. You fear them because they seem to have power of some nature. But if you knew of your death, you would be able to see which of those people truly have power, and few people do.

Agnes Whistling Elk
Medicine Woman

October 31

You Are Limitless

This rock is that part of you that believes in being honest. Yet only one who has shattered the egg of truth and falsehood can be honest. You mother that egg as though it contained a precious child—you brood over counterfeit eggs. Can you throw these children away one by one? You better. You must realize that you are not free. Walk the sacred path and hatch the limitless egg.

Agnes Whistling Elk
Medicine Woman

November 1

Fly Through the Center of the Spiral

To keep you from the formless unknowable, the mind helps you develop addictions that bleed off your life force. We stay in form when we throw away the power of our spirit. Whenever we develop an addiction, whether it is alcohol or depression, it has only one effect and that is the effect of spirit sleep. When your spirit sleeps it means you are losing life force and you go further and further away from the center of the spiral. You die a little with every addiction. It is the opposite end of the arrow from enlightenment. Fly through the center of the spiral and witness your depression. It is only a trick of the mind to keep you in earthly bondage.

Ruby Plenty Chiefs
Crystal Woman

November 2

Wisdom of Understanding

This is a long path that we have walked together. It is a ribbon, a shiny ribbon of time, that goes through history. You need only to follow that ribbon to reach your illumination. We do not know how long we all have together, but never will there be a true separation. We are part of each other now, through the wisdom of understanding.

Ruby Plenty Chiefs
Shakkai, Woman of the Sacred Garden

November 3

Stand Your Ground

Everyone belongs to a spirit clan. Some spirit clans are visible and some are invisible. You have to recognize your spirit clan, and that's not so easy. An act of power is required. If you do an act of power, you'll be tested by one spirit clan. When you meet the test, you must stand motionless. Throw your shoulders back and be proud of what you've accomplished. Let the representation of the spirit clan test you and, whatever you do, don't run away in terror.

Agnes Whistling Elk
Flight of the Seventh Moon

Listen with Your Heart

Within each of us there is a being that we must come to know. That spirit in you talks to the plant spirits. Close your eyes and listen with your heart.

Zoila
Jaguar Woman

Balance of Power

When women fall in love, they want to give away their power. We all come into this earthwalk to heal our femaleness. Man or woman, it makes no difference. Women come into this round knowing a great truth. But like most women, you couldn't define what you knew. Some women become indifferent to this knowledge. You wanted to understand this knowledge. This is what brought you here. You found me to help you. When men come into this round, they do not know. If they are lucky, they realize they have to find a woman to teach them. Men do not know how to live. Women must teach them that. But first women have to take their own power and heal themselves. They imitate men like a mockingbird imitates a crow. Once they do that, it's all over. It's all wrong. Men and women both lose and become weak. When you are a goddess, then you can mate with your god successfully, and only then.

Agnes Whistling Elk
Jaguar Woman

November 6

Observe Your Behavior

Observe your own behavior. Look down on yourself like a noble eagle in the sky. See how foolish you are, and forgive yourself. You are only human. See what the thunderchiefs see. Against the grandeur of the sky we all shrink in importance.

Agnes Whistling Elk
Star Woman

November 7

Life Is a Dream

We live in a dream. Dreams are like clouds dotting the sky. Sometimes with power we create a great wind and sometimes those clouds bump into each other. At that moment of collision something new becomes possible. You as a shamaness have the opportunity to confront the dream. At that moment you can change the agreements that you have with your reality and you can change reality.

Ruby Plenty Chiefs
Windhorse Woman

November 8

Listen to Your Scouts

The shaman person never makes a mistake. A shaman woman knows how to send her scouts out from her moon lodge to look things over. When she gets to where she's going, she knows what to expect, because her scouts have already been there and told her everything.

Agnes Whistling Elk
Medicine Woman

November 9

Step into the Mystery

If you speak to a person who is standing in a powerless position and tell her to take her power, she becomes frightened because you are implying change. She must take a step into the mystery of the unknown to become powerful.

Agnes Whistling Elk
Flight of the Seventh Moon

November 10

Between the Lines

Always look for the truth beyond the words.

Agnes Whistling Elk
Jaguar Woman

November 11

Feel the Heartbeat of Mother Earth

Agnes dipped her fingers into one of the clay pots. She touched the center of my head where my part was and she drew a line down the center.

"This paint is red for woman," she said. "That red line unites you with the earth, where everything dwells and is fertile."

Agnes Whistling Elk
Medicine Woman

November 12

Muse-Female

Agnes told me that the basket was woven by dreamers and represented an unspeakable void—the womb in woman. It is law that all things must be born in woman, even things invented by men. All the stars were born from the void, and the void is woman. Creation invented the male to balance that. It said, I'll put a man inside her. In a man is the muse-female. Agnes said that men have taken the void and said it was theirs, and that as a result our Mother Earth is now in a state of great imbalance.

Lynn
Medicine Woman

November 13

Wake Up the Spirits

The spirits sleep in all the named and nameless things. They are fast asleep in everything. Yet there may not have been a ceremony here for the last thousand years. To us it seems like a long time, but it is but a breath in forever. The spirits of a power place wait and they slumber. When you, as a shaman, arrive, the first thing you must do is wake up the spirits and make them stand up. Remember that a ceremony is only as powerful as the person giving it. If you can't wake up the spirits of a place, you may as well pack it in and go home.

Twin Dreamers
Star Woman

November 14

Living Close to Power

Mother Earth has a lot to do with dreaming. Your connection to her is important, how you have honored and given away to her. Many of our people think when you travel above the clouds and you look down and everything is white, they think everything is the same, you know? People of the spirit understand each other around the world. The gods live in the sky. They speak the same language. Power is in the rocks and the earth. That means that when we take something from the earth, our mother, we must return that energy in a ceremony, with honor. Then the power stays happy and never leaves. Power only leaves when you take and never give back. Power knows me, she helps me. She's beginning to recognize you, too. You're living close to her now.

Ginevee
Crystal Woman

Are You a Woman?

Agnes suddenly asked, a change in her mood, "Are you a woman?"

"Yes."

"Are you a woman when you are naked?"

"Yes," I answered.

"Do you have a vagina?"

"Yes."

I couldn't imagine what she meant by this line of questioning.

"Do you menstruate?"

"Yes."

"We didn't know. In the native world it is called your moon. It is your time of greatest power. Last night we had to make sure."

Agnes Whistling Elk and Lynn
Medicine Woman

November 16

A Lonely Dream

I looked at every woman there, and with tears of inexplicable joy I realized that something within me recognized each and every woman. I also saw the reincarnation of women's lonely dream upon the earth. With this came the terrible strain of knowledge, and I saw the irrevocable consequences of action. Into this vision I was drawn—into this mysterious joy of being, this mirror of the joyous and brutal facts of life and death, pain and pleasure.

Lynn
Flight of the Seventh Moon

November 17

Losing Your Way

Many people carry around a bagful of stones, a whole bagful of conceptions, that weights them down, that limits their growth and puts a fence around their consciousness so that they cannot see beyond that fence. It is important to have ideas and feelings, because with those ideas and feelings you create mirrors, and those mirrors are great teachers for you. But when you are full of ideas, those ideas give you what you think is the right to pass judgment on what other people do. That is one of the greatest wasting processes of life that I know. People do a lot of that and that is a tragedy, because they get lost in their judgments. They get lost in their criticism, and they forget where they're going, why they're alive, and what their purpose on earth is. They will tell you what their purpose is, but in reality they have lost their way, and they are frightened.

Agnes Whistling Elk
Shakkai, Woman of the Sacred Garden

November 18

You Are Part of a Greater Circle

You are still learning the way. One day soon you will understand the meaning of the Sisterhood of the Shields. I cannot explain it to you any better. Simply realize that in your earthwalk, each shield belongs to a larger single shield. You have to become a master of the shields, and when you do, you will discover the warrioress's destiny.

Ruby Plenty Chiefs
Flight of the Seventh Moon

November 19

Be Receptive to the Great Spirit

"I feel an emptiness, Agnes, whenever I sit here by the creek."

"That emptiness is a prayer. You are making a place for the Great Spirit to live inside you."

Lynn and Agnes Whistling Elk
The Woman of Wyrrd

November 20

Let the Plants Teach You

Go out into the garden and sit with the plants. Just sit in silence with them. Talk to them and let them speak to you. The flowers that have a fragrance are asking you to notice them. They are more highly evolved than the blooms without it. The scent brings you to them and enables them to evolve and become more like you, more human. That is the purpose of fragrance. The rose is highly evolved, because it has such magnificent form as well as a heady scent. They are asking for your love, and they need your light.

Grandmother
The Woman of Wyrrd

November 21

Struggle Is a Challenge to Grow

This is a time of great planetary change. Many of the great time calendars are ending now because we are entering a new age of wisdom. We have the possibility of creating a new world of heightened understanding. We live in a time of great vision. The great libraries of knowledge will be opened to many from different paths and religions. There is much for you to learn, but truth is never reached without struggle on the human path.

Ani
Windhorse Woman

November 22

Look for Power in Unlikely Places

Learn how to see. You have taken too many things for granted. Your vision is but a glimpse. Everything is disguised.

Agnes Whistling Elk
Medicine Woman

November 23

Becoming Is Only the Beginning

"There is something inside me, Agnes, that makes me not ever want to stop learning. Somehow, to come to the end of my apprenticeship makes me think of death, makes me feel like there's an end to life's magic in some way. It frightens me."

"That is why so many people enjoy living on the edge. They dwell in the world of becoming, and never completely accomplish, not really. They never truly become. They are afraid to own what they have accomplished, because somehow that would mean that they are finished. In actuality, becoming is only the beginning. Perhaps that is what you need to see, my daughter."

Lynn and Agnes Whistling Elk
Shakkai, Woman of the Sacred Garden

November 24

Sacred Dance

If you had looked away from your own reflection, no matter how horrible, you would have fallen from the butterfly tree forever. You would have fallen back into endless sleep. When men and women fall away from their own vision of sacredness, their culture falls away into sleep with them. Sacred vision contains the balance of light and dark. The positive and negative need each other for creation, for the sacred dance to take place.

Butterfly Woman
Jaguar Woman

November 25

Sit in Stillness

Only within the void does truth enter. Within emptiness you become pregnant with what you are searching for.

Ruby Plenty Chiefs
Windhorse Woman

November 26

Gather Personal Power

Everyone is born belonging to a circle. There is no power until you have completed your circle. The task of the huntress, the task of the warrioress, is the gathering of enough personal power to be able to join with your circle once you find them.

Agnes Whistling Elk
Flight of the Seventh Moon

November 27

Know Your Wildness

In the beginning when the world was formed, the chiefs sent the wolf cubs out to explore and measure the world. They went down all the trails of the world. Wolf medicine means measure. Wolves are good mathematicians if they want to be. If you are one with your medicine you can never be tricked, because you've been down all the trails. It's a very powerful and hypnotic medicine.

Agnes Whistling Elk
Medicine Woman

November 28

Follow the Light

We in the Sisterhood must remain hidden and secret. To be able to dream, to work on other levels daily, to help balance the energies of Mother Earth, we must never leave our center. It requires an extraordinary effort to maintain this shaman stance. To be known would be to lose our power. That is the truth of it.

Higher wisdom has always been held in secret to protect it for those who are prepared for it. When light shines, the darkness encroaches on the edges of brilliance to define it and give the light an even truer definition.

Agnes Whistling Elk
The Woman of Wyrrd

November 29

Never Underestimate Your Enemies

In your trust and innocence, never underestimate your enemy. In the west within your introspection, estimate and recognize any possible move your enemy might make. In the north, in your wisdom, know that an enemy can assume any potential. In illumination in the east, realize that a self army never exhausts itself in any manner. Standing in the center, you can see that a great war chief knows all the territories, inner and outer, in which armies exist. Remember that ignorance is your greatest enemy.

Agnes Whistling Elk
Flight of the Seventh Moon

November 30

Receive Spirit

To get the marriage basket, you must become the proper receptacle. You must ripen your void so that the energy of what you want, in this case the basket, will flow magnetically toward your belly. You must become what she wants so that there is no separating you. When you think of yourself as a separate entity, you will obstruct that current and the basket will defeat you.

Agnes Whistling Elk
Medicine Woman

December 1

You Are from the Stars

"Agnes, what happened to the Star Nations? Did they come and then just leave?"

"No one knows for sure, my daughter. They came from the stars, and to the stars they returned, but we think they have brought back their knowledge from time to time, that they have manifested this knowledge through people who have walked the earth. These people have known where to find wisdom."

Lynn and Agnes Whistling Elk
The Woman of Wyrrd

December 2

You Have a Choice

Just as there is a part of you that likes to just be, there is a part of you that likes to do things. The important thing is that you experience the difference between these two parts of yourself. But also, it is important for you to understand that there is a choice. You have the choice to do too much or just enough, and you also have the choice just to be.

Grandmother
The Woman of Wyrrd

December 3

Walk in Balance

If it is meat you are hunting, you must never waste any of it—not even the bones. Hunted meat has a spirit. It has a big spirit that will make you strong. The sweet meat of the slave animals holds no responsibility to you. It tastes sweet, but it makes you fat and indolent. You have to be balanced in the physical world and balanced in the spirit world. Then those two balances have to again be balanced.

Agnes Whistling Elk
Medicine Woman

December 4

Look Forward to Change

All things are present within a single moment. Your final step is contained within your first step. Life is a circle. The beginning is always the end.

Agnes Whistling Elk
Windhorse Woman

December 5

Kinship with the Wind

All emotions have a kinship with the wind. You must let these emotions go through you and travel on their way. Otherwise, you magnetize bad energy, which is what you do by clutching your unresolved sadness.

Agnes Whistling Elk
Star Woman

December 6

Your Life Is a Teaching

I can walk through a gathering and snake them into confusion. I can get inside your head and turn you around, and you don't know what you're doing. If I can confuse you, then you know you must get stronger. My life is a teaching. I stay in the simple because it's the most sensible. I'm not bragging. It's just what is.

Ruby Plenty Chiefs
Flight of the Seventh Moon

December 7

Renegade

I am a renegade. I have been a ronin all of my life. I speak for no one except spirit, and I will teach you the way of light, the way of great illumination. All you must do is listen with your heart. In a way your pain has brought you to me, and it is good. Without your pain, you could not bear the joy that is soon to be yours. Your pain has given you depth, a way to open your spirit. Never think that there is not a reason for everything that happens.

Shakkai
Shakkai, Woman of the Sacred Garden

December 8

The Creative One

Realize la Ultima Madre, realize who you are, and become who you are. Realize you belong to Rainbow Mother and embody her. The soul she has is the soul you have. For you, she is la Ultima Madre. You are the creative one who dances with dreams and visions.

Zoila
Jaguar Woman

December 9

Power Comes from Woman

You must remember in your heart that a tree is no less alive than you are. But people do not understand that. They have forgotten the source of power. They have forgotten that power comes from woman, from this great Mother Earth. You understand in your heart and you protect her, but to protect her is to protect yourself.

Grandmother
The Woman of Wyrrd

December 10

The First Lesson of Power

The first lesson of power is that we are alone. The last lesson of power is that we are all one.

Grandmother
The Woman of Wyrrd

December 11

You Are of the Earth

You were brought between the rattles last night, the mother rattle and the night-eagle rattle, two irresistible forces. Your life was spun like a web between them. In a moment, they could have torn you apart, but it was from them that you drew your power. There is no part of you that is not of this mother planet. The mother bear dances with the white-plumed arrows, and last night the points of the arrows met. The Mother Earth mingled her energy with yours. The earth is a reservoir of energy. You merged with that elemental force, and you are that force.

Agnes Whistling Elk
Medicine Woman

December 12
Great Mother

When we understand the great mothers in us, we can live in harmony and help fulfill each other's destinies.

Zoila
Jaguar Woman

December 13
Everything Is Your Teacher

Every book is rewritten by the reader. If you read a book, it becomes your personal teacher. You bring to it what you are.

Agnes Whistling Elk
Flight of the Seventh Moon

December 14

Remember Your Dreams

"In other words the dreamers have come to me in the second round and have taken me between the worlds?"

"That is right, but you don't have the power yet to remember anything but your dreams."

"But why are they coming to me?"

"Because consciously or unconsciously you have made a bid for power."

"In other words, be careful what you ask for?"

Lynn and Agnes Whistling Elk
Medicine Woman

December 15

Ride the Wave

Life is like a wave that rolls into shore. Then it floats back and disappears into the greater sea, until it peaks and comes up again with even greater strength. Life and death are like that.

Ani
Windhorse Woman

December 16

Finding Your Way Home

Our relationship is about illumination. It is about finding your way home. Our relationship is like a tiny turquoise bead along this trail. It is just a signpost. It is just a piece of the love, the greater love, that you will be immersed in later on in your lifetimes.

Agnes Whistling Elk
Shakkai, Woman of the Sacred Garden

December 17

Yours Is the Path of Heart

"Lynn, you are at the beginning. I, as your teacher and advisor, am at the beginning also. All life and the life of a shaman woman are at the beginning. One day you will come to see this. Your way is born here." Agnes placed her fist over her heart. "Here is the light that came out of darkness. Here dwell the secrets that are like good food that will nourish you. Here is where words are born, words capable of giving you the great lie and the great truth."

Agnes Whistling Elk
Flight of the Seventh Moon

December 18

A Mourner Doll

A mourner doll is you. It contains within its belly all your pain, greed, sorrow, and fears. In other words, it is a doll built and divined as a tangible expression of your intangible addictions. It is made of your crazy winds, your negativity, the impulses that have crippled your spirit. A mourner doll is your death. It is made for your transformation from one life to another. It is a conveyance, a canoe, a bridge. It becomes a symbol on the altar of your metamorphosis from your immature self lodge to your medicine lodge, where your sacred things are kept in this lifetime. These dolls represent the powers within you. Your life power and your death power. What you choose not to look at in life rules your life. That is why the mourner doll is so important, and why I want you to make her first. Fashion her out of the darkest depths within your own spirit. Build her of your twisted and broken dreams, the things you want to bury and be done with forever. The mourner doll represents your death and a process of mourning for what is about to die.

Agnes Whistling Elk
Star Woman

December 19

Life Is a Miracle

Life is a miracle. The world is as it should be. It is so hard for us to find our way through the mud, to celebrate the innocence and the seeds of knowledge that we plant there. We must foster those seeds. We must find those seeds and give them life.

Shakkai
Shakkai, Woman of the Sacred Garden

December 20

Isle of the Mortals

Smallness is power, because in smallness we condense and contain the vastness of the universe within a single seed, and from that seed is born all of life. It is in your smallness that you have been able to go through the tiny neck of your sacred hu, your beautiful gourd, into the garden of the immortals where all life is possible. You are never born and you never die. It is on these islands of the immortals that you will live forever. It is love that has brought you here. It is the teachings of the path of heart, the expansion of your soul with goodness and joy, that have brought you here, to this sacred sea.

Shakkai
Shakkai, Woman of the Sacred Garden

WINTER

December 21

Reflect Beauty

Reflection is a beautiful word. Reflection means thinking about things in the past or the future. To reflect does not necessarily mean to think about things that really exist. Reflection also means a mirroring.

Ani
Windhorse Woman

December 22

Remember Who You Are

Out of darkness, intolerance, prejudice, and imbalance, you are working to reveal the power and sacredness in all women. You, and many others of our sex, are beginning to remember who they are. You do not yet remember completely who you are, but soon you will know.

Jaguar Woman
Jaguar Woman

December 23

Child of the Mystery

Lynn, you have entered the womb of the great mystery. You saw many things that you will remember only slowly because it is still beyond your personal power to know. You have come again from that great womb. Through that birth you will know the great mystery, for you are of it. You are the child of that mystery and from that birth comes the deathless life. You will remember the details as you begin to identify with the void that is woman. In you and in a man, you sit in the center of the self shield in the place of the grandmothers. You gave up your lies. We all live a lie until we are reborn through the void. And when you remember it all, you will be a shaman woman who shows others that there is no death.

Agnes Whistling Elk
Flight of the Seventh Moon

December 24

Love

Think about how you can change when you are in love. Love is a word for transformation. When you say, "I love you," you are saying, "I transform you." But since you alone can transform no one, what you are really saying is, "I transform myself and my vision." I am always living in the lodge of love and I share it with you.

Agnes Whistling Elk
Flight of the Seventh Moon

December 25

Beingness

Tonight you will learn that the Great Spirit and the Great Mother have not given you life that you would be alone. To know that you are truly alone is the first step on a long journey to self-discovery on the path to power. The next step is to learn that you are linked with the universe, that you live in all the lodges of the universe. Life flowers and nourishes itself from within. Beingness has realized itself within you.

Agnes Whistling Elk
Star Woman

December 26

Celebrate Your Strength

I am full. It is an expression among my people. It means, "I have eaten. I am full." It has nothing to do with food. We don't go around thanking each other for things. There is only one to thank, the noble Great Spirit. It means I am full inside for what we have shared. I feel good. We have only one gift, and that is to choose our death. You say thank you in your world. Thank you is a lie, and I advise you never to say it again. You may say it as a ritual, but never say thank you to any man—it robs you of power. There is only one exception. When you truly see the Great Spirit in another—then you may address that Spirit in thanks and celebration.

Agnes Whistling Elk
Medicine Woman

December 27

In Silence There Is Divinity

Silence is where the Great Spirit lives. He does not live in language. That's why you love animals, nature, and horses so much; because there are no words between you, only silence. You transmit your love for them from the heart and not from your mind in words. In silence there is divinity.

Agnes Whistling Elk
Windhorse Woman

December 28

Open Your Heart

Think of your body as a road map. When seen this way, it speaks of your spiritual, emotional, and psychic development. When I look at you, I can see where your holes are. As you know, I see where you hold your energy and where you leak it out. When a person holds energy in the heart I know that that person has trauma there, is afraid to open up and love, and could develop any number of heart problems.

Agnes Whistling Elk
Jaguar Woman

December 29

Path of Balance

The path of illumination is the path of balance, the path of balance with one foot in the material world and one foot securely rooted in the spiritual world. Many people today who are on this path, the path of spirit, are filled with anger from their childhoods. They never deal with that anger, and they throw away the physical life out of a need to reject the pain of their earlier life, and they call themselves spiritual. But they sabotage themselves at every turn. They hold up a spirit shield, but their feet are not planted on bedrock. Their feet are planted in quicksand, and spiritual power will eventually overwhelm them. Then one day they will have to hear the voice of the great teachers, and that voice will tell them that they need to go back and learn to walk in balance. For everything you do spiritually, you need to strengthen your body as well.

Agnes Whistling Elk
Shakkai, Woman of the Sacred Garden

December 30

Wake Up

Everyone has what he or she needs, the mirrors. Each of us has asked, before being born, for everything needed. The problem is, when we are born, we become caught in the dream. We are born into a kind of sleep. To become enlightened is to wake up from that dream.

Agnes Whistling Elk
The Woman of Wyrrd

December 31

Sing Your Creation Song

Long ago, the sacred grandparents said that there was no day and no sun. The Great Spirit was the only. The Great Spirit was the center. The Great Spirit was the source without end. The grandparents told the daughter winds to blow the macrocosm into existence. The Great Spirit hid and divided up into niece and nephew. Together they sang the creation song. Everything vibrates with this voice—the universe, the galaxies, the sun and the earth. Light and darkness and all things are but a song of the Great Spirit. The Great Spirit is sleeping in all the named and nameless things.

Agnes Whistling Elk
Medicine Woman

For the last ten years, I've been describing my learning and my path. It has been a joy to do this. In continuing my journey, I would be grateful if you would share your insights with me.

Please write me at:
Lynn Andrews
2934½ Beverly Glen Circle
Box 378
Los Angeles, CA 90077

Please send me your name and address so I can share any new information with you.